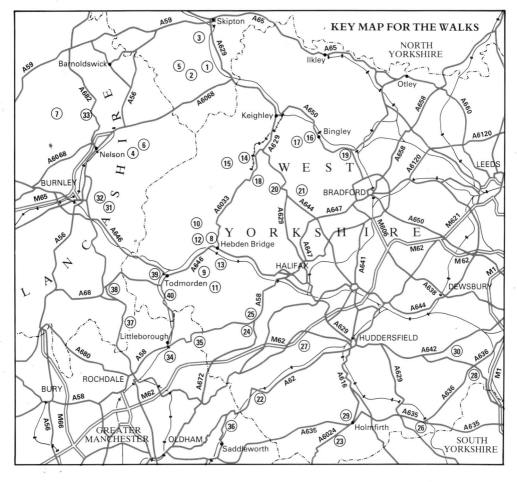

KEY MAP FOR THE WALKS

Key to maps

Scale 1:25000

0 ———————————————— 1 mile
0 ———————————————— 1 km

All maps are drawn on a north axis, ie. with north at the top

▬▬▬ Major road	++++ Railway (BR)	W
——— Other road	Ⓐ Description in text	183m Sp
- - - - Track or footpath	❈ Viewpoint	P Pa
- - - - Route of walk	▲ Summit	🚌 Bu

WALKING IN THE SOUTH PENNINES

The Pennines and our freedom of access to them have become highly emotive symbols for the rambling community in England. These hills and mountains, forming the backbone of England, have helped millions of people living and working in the industrial towns of the North to endure the dark days of the Industrial Revolution. The high moors still give a taste of freedom, while the intimate, deep wooded valleys allow close contact with nature. The South Pennines provide outstandingly beautiful scenery within easy reach of a vast population. Access is made very easy by a commendably cheap, efficient, frequent and integrated system of public transport.

The best way to discover this area is, of course, on foot. Take to the hills, moors and valleys and you will find fresh air, natural peace, fine views – and the footpaths that lead to them. Even our industrial heritage now adds interest to many walks, for example the towpaths of the three trans-Pennine canals provide easy, peaceful strolls for urban dwellers.

So often our most magnificent countryside is inaccessible, either through lack of public transport or by rights of way going unclaimed or neglected by unsympathetic local authorities or landowners. As long as walkers keep to the rights of way or concessionary routes, they are made to feel really welcome in the South Pennines.

1 SHAPING THE LAND

The landscape of the South Pennines has been shaped over the past 350 million years by the elements and, more recently, by man. Clear seas once covered this part of Britain, inhabited by tiny creatures whose shells have since become limestone. Earth movements led to a huge river draining the area, carrying grits, sands and silts to its delta. These now form layers of Millstone grit which outcrop to add drama to the scenery. Tropical vegetation then flourished and decayed to form coal.

Massive movements at the end of the Carboniferous period resulted in a major north-south mountain fold, with a secondary fold at a right angle through Rossendale. The Ice Age brought ice sheets pushing boulders from the Lake District and Scotland, and dammed valleys which subsequently filled with lakes. The Calder Valley was deepened considerably by water overflowing from East Lancashire and Airedale. The result is high sided valleys and waterfalls with tributary streams eroding deeper valleys or cloughs.

Peat covers the high moors to a depth of 30 feet (9m), a result of man's deforestation during the past 4000 years. Resultant changes in the soil structure have resulted in only the poorest forms of vegetation being able to survive. Growing trees and plants normally absorb minerals in the soil, replacing them each autumn with their fallen leaves. The intervention of man has broken this cycle. As populations moved down to the lower terraces, the upland moors were used for sheep grazing and their heather was burned to aid grouse rearing.

There are four distinct areas in the South Pennines. **The uplands** were the home of prehistoric man and are now a source of peat, stone and coal. Valleys here are increasingly being flooded to supply the towns with water. **Hillside terraces** were farmed during the Middle Ages and villages are found on them. The textile industry has its origins here. **The cloughs**, or narrow tributary valleys, were ideal locations for water powered mills. These old mill sites are now hidden by the delightful trees that have survived on their steep sides. **The main valleys** finally became the home of the textile industry and its workers as coal was used to make steam power and canals and railways were constructed to carry it.

2 THE INDUSTRIAL HERITAGE

Farming in the South Pennines has always consisted mainly of grazing sheep, although until recently few of the people could afford to eat the meat which was produced. The staple grain was oats until cheap corn from elsewhere became easily available in the mid 19th century. Communications prior to the Industrial Revolution consisted of long distance paths or packhorse routes, often used for the import of lime desirable for the area's acid soil. The poor soil encouraged farmers to diversify, with the manufacture of cloth providing just such an opportunity. The 16th century saw the rise of the 'Yeoman Clothier', entrepreneurial middlemen who supplied raw wool to self-employed handloom weavers and collected their finished pieces to sell. As the textile industry rose in importance special cottages were built for weavers.

Slivers of wool were spun into a yarn on a spinning wheel. They had to be washed and 'wuzzed' dry before being woven. The next stage was fulling, to make the cloth thick, warm and windproof. This involved soaking the piece in stale urine and trampling it underfoot. The cloth was cleaned with fullers earth and stretched to dry on 'tenterhooks'.

People began settling in weaving communities. Turnpike roads were built and piece or cloth halls were erected for trading. Tremendous expansion took place from 1770 to 1840, reflecting the growth of the British Empire. Mills or factories replaced the cottage industry, firstly with the aid of waterpower, then with steam. Coal was brought by canal. A growing population led to more land being used for dairy herds and large areas were enclosed. New machinery and the factory environment turned people into employees and town dwellers. Religious enthusiasm was strong, with John Wesley (1703-91), the evangelist and founder of Methodism, frequently visiting the area. He observed that child labour was a 'means of preventing youthful vice'.

The coming of the steam engine and the canals and railways emphasised these changes, creating bigger mills and bigger towns. Energy was infectious and specialisation grew. Living conditions for the workers were so harsh and squalid that their need for improvement could not be ignored. Building societies were formed in places such as Halifax as a form of self-help. Some mill owners, like Titus Salt of Saltaire and 'Honest John' Fielden of Todmorden, cared for their workers and urged reforms in working conditions. Civic pride was expressed in grand public buildings. A reduction in factory hours allowed some time for recreation and the people exercised their freedom to roam the hills. The textile industry has declined, and the footpaths have become a major tourist asset, with nature reclaiming old industrial land.

3 BRONTË COUNTRY

It was Charlotte Brontë who wrote: 'Speak of the North – a lonely moor, silent and still and trackless lies'. The most vivid descriptions were by her sister Emily in *Wuthering Heights*. Charlotte was to write of Emily that 'there is not a knoll of heather, not a branch of fern, not a young bilberry leaf, not a fluttering lark or linnet, but reminds me of her'. As for her other sister, the author of *The Tenant of Wildfell Hall*, 'the distant prospects were Anne's delight, and when I look round, she is in the blue tints, the pale mists, the waves and shadows of the horizons'. The Brontës made this a literary landscape. They came to it at Thornton but soon moved to Haworth, where, according to Mrs Gaskell, Charlotte Brontë's biographer, there was a 'wild, rough population. Their accost is curt, their accent and tone of speech is blunt and harsh . . . Their feelings are not easily roused, but their duration is lasting. Hence their is much close friendship and faithful service . . . From the same cause come also enduring grudges, in some cases amounting to hatred, which occasionally have been bequeathed from generation to generation'.

4 SAFETY FIRST

The walks in this guide are intended for the enjoyment of all, including those with no prior experience and who possess a minimum of equipment. Comfortable walking shoes and a lightweight waterproof anorak will be all you need for the majority of them. Even the high level walks are quite safe *if approached with common sense*, but before undertaking these, there are precautions you *must* take.

Always remember that there is the potential danger of a sudden change in the weather and be prepared for this (see the 'Weathercall' information in section **9**). The climb to the top of Pendle Hill, for example, means a 5°F (2.8C) drop in temperature (without allowing for the wind-chill factor). You can easily get lost in mist on the upland moors when the valley bottoms are warm and sunny, so be sure to notice landmarks when ascending so that you can find your way down easily.

Good, sound equipment is also essential for the high level walks. Walking boots or stout walking shoes are the most important item – don't wear training shoes, wellington boots or sandals. Several layers of clothing are preferable to one heavy jersey. Avoid jeans (which are very uncomfortable if soaked) and carry a pair of trousers (track suit trousers are ideal) if you're wearing shorts. After boots, an anorak is the next most important item. It should keep out the wind and be waterproof. A warm hat is essential and gloves are also recommended. Wear what is necessary, and stop to put on extra clothing as required. Always carry some spare emergency clothing, a torch and batteries, plenty of high energy foods (chocolate bars, for example) and some drink.

A 1:25,000 scale map is essential for high moorland walks. Practise relating your route to the map and be able to give a grid reference in case you have to fetch help for a friend. If you are caught in mist, a good compass is reliable - your own sense of direction is not. Practise using a map and compass in easy conditions before you have to rely on them when things are difficult.

Plan your walk allowing plenty of time to complete it, including having a picnic and enjoying the views. Notice bad weather escape routes. Don't venture onto the high level walks alone, and tell someone where you are going and when you should be back. Regrettably, a spate of thefts from walkers' cars nationally means that it may no longer be wise to write where you are going on a note displayed inside the windscreen of your car. Remember that heavy rain can make streams impassable. Don't attempt to cross such streams in spate. If in doubt, turn back. Avoid jumping dangerously from boulder to boulder.

Walk with a steady rhythm. Look to place your feet on level ground and let the whole of the foot contact the ground, not just the toe. Take short steps on uneven ground and take care not to dislodge loose stones onto walkers below. If in a party, walk to the pace of the slowest member and keep the party together but in single file. Appoint a 'rear person' to ensure no one is left behind. Don't overtake the leader but do take note of your route so that you could lead if necessary. Remember to carry a whistle for emergency distress signals (six blasts per minute) and use a torch for signalling in the dark. Note where the nearest telephone is should you need to make a 999 call and always have some 10p coins available for other calls.

5 WILDLIFE

Remnants of the great upland forests which once covered the South Pennines remain in the narrow sheltered valleys known as cloughs. Silver birch, oak and hazel still survive here, although the Scots pine, which would have also been present on what is now bare moorland, are no longer to be found.

Red and grey squirrels frequent the cloughs. The great spotted woodpecker (*dendropocos major*) also prefers such broad-leaved woodland. It can be distinguished by its 'drumming' noise. Look also for the tree creeper, searching for insects as it runs up tree trunks. The moisture in the woodland attracts frogs, which find water here in which to spawn. Dragonflies dart on the wing while, at your feet, wood ants build tunnels and chambers inside cone shaped ant hills. Such ants control the looper caterpillar, and stop it from defoliating the woodland.

Up on the moors, red grouse (*lagopus lagopus*) find cover in the heather. Drainage operations have resulted in the insectivorous sundew and bog asphodel not being as common as they were at the time of the Brontës, but wild flowers such as the purple foxglove and yellow bird's-foot trefoil can still delight the eye.

6 RIGHTS OF WAY

All the walks in this guide follow established rights of way. Always keep to the official paths and rights of way, remembering always that there is no general right of access to the hills in this area. If you have a dog, please remember to keep it on a lead or, better still, leave it behind if you are likely to encounter sheep. The Animals Act (1971) states that dogs considered to be endangering livestock may be shot. The Protection of Livestock Act (1953) makes it an offence to permit a dog to worry livestock, with a maximum penalty of 200. Worrying includes being at large in a field in which there are sheep. The definitive maps and statements that are legal proofs of public rights of way are held by County Councils and Metropolitan District Councils, as highway authorities. Further information on rights of way is available from the Ramblers' Association, 1-5 Wandsworth Road, London, SW8 2LJ or from Countryside Services of the local authority concerned.

7 THE COUNTRY CODE

Enjoy the countryside and respect its life and work.

Guard against all risk of fire.

Leave gates as you find them.

Keep your dog under proper control.

Keep to public paths.

Use gates and stiles to cross fences, hedges and walls.

Leave livestock, crops and machinery alone.

Take your litter home.

Help to keep all water clean.

Protect wildlife, plants and trees.

Take special care on country roads.

Make no unnecessary noise.

8 PUBLIC TRANSPORT

The South Pennines are, for the most part, a shining example of how our public transport system can be made into a great public asset. Services here are designed to facilitate walking in the countryside during leisure periods. A comprehensive network covers the whole area and services are frequent, even on Sundays. Fares are kept at sensibly low levels and there are many bargain tickets for holiday-makers and day-trippers. If you can reach the start of a walk by bus, this is clearly stated on that walk, although no route numbers are mentioned if the walk is served by a multitude of buses from all major centres. The area is easy to reach from other parts, with Leeds the best centre for trains both within the South Pennines and from and to other places on British Rail's Inter-city network. See the next section for information and telephone numbers.

It is not uncommon even for drivers who have towed a caravan to the area to forsake their cars when in West Yorkshire. Most of the walks in this guide can be reached by public transport and are within the area covered by the 'Metrocard'.

9 USEFUL ADDRESSES

West Yorkshire Passenger Transport Executive
Metro House, West Parade, Wakefield, WF1 1NS. Tel. 0924 378234/375555.
Lancashire County Council, Public Transport Enquiries
Winckley House, PO Box 9, Cross Street, Preston, PR1 8RD. Tel. 0772 264563/263333.

Greater Manchester Passenger Transport Executive
PO Box 429, 9 Portland Street, Piccadilly Gardens, Manchester, M60 1HX. Tel. 061 228 6400/7811.
Keighley & Worth Valley Railway Society
Haworth Station, Keighley, West Yorkshire, BD22 8NJ. Tel. 0535 43629 (talking timetable), 45214 (general).
Tourist Information Centres
Bradford City Hall, Channing Way, Bradford, W. Yorkshire BD1 1HY. Tel. 0274 753678.
Burnley Burnley Mechanics, Manchester Road, Burnley, Lancashire BB11 1JA. Tel. 0282 30055.
Halifax The Piece Hall, Westgate, Halifax, W. Yorkshire HX1 1RE. Tel. 0422 68725.
Haworth 2 - 4 West Lane, Haworth, W. Yorkshire B22 8EF. Tel. 0535 42329.
Hebden Bridge 1 Bridge Gate, Hebden Bridge, W. Yorkshire HX7 1JP. Tel. 0422 843831.
Holmfirth 50 - 51 Huddersfield Road, Holmfirth, W. Yorkshire HD7 1JP. Tel. 0484 684992.
Huddersfield 3 Albion Street, Huddersfield, W. Yorkshire HD1 2NW. Tel. 0484 22133.
Ilkley Station Road, Ilkley, W. Yorkshire LS29 8HA. Tel. 0943 602319.
Oldham 84 Union Street, Oldham, Gt Manchester OL1 1DN. Tel. 061-678 4654.
Pendle 20 Scotland Road, Nelson, Lancashire BB9 9SZ. Tel. 0282 692890.
Rochdale The Clock Tower, Town Hall, Rochdale, Lancashire OL16 1AB. Tel. 0706 356592.
Rossendale 41 - 45 Kay Street, Rawtenstall, Lancashire BB4 7LS. Tel. 0706 217777.
Saddleworth Saddleworth Museum, High Street, Uppermill, Gt Manchester OL3 6HJ. Tel. 04577 4093.
Skipton Victoria Square, Skipton, N. Yorkshire BD23 1JF. Tel. 0756 2809.
Sowerby Bridge 40 Town Hall Street, Sowerby Bridge, W. Yorkshire HX6 2EA. Tel. 0422 835326.
Todmorden 15 Burnley Road, Todmorden, Lancashire OL14 7BU. Tel. 0706 818181.
SCOSPA (The Standing Conference of South Pennine Authorities), Jacob's Well, Manchester Road, Bradford, BD1 5RN.
The Brontë Society
Brontë Parsonage, Haworth, near Keighley, W. Yorkshire BD22 8DR. Tel. 0535 42323.
Weathercall: Lancashire: Tel. 0898 500 416, Yorkshire: Tel. 0898 500 417.

Walk 1

CONONLEY

0   1 mile

0   1 km

4.3 miles (6.9 km) Moderate

A traditional Airedale mill village is set at the foot of a hill riddled with old lead mines. Above the mines is the site of a gibbet or gallows. The view across the Aire valley is excellent, extending to Skipton, behind which rise the tops of Flasby Fell and Barden Moor. Further along you will see Earl Crag to the south. This is a grand place to walk.

1 *Start from Cononley's station on British Rail's Airedale Line between Leeds and Skipton. The no. 666 bus between Bradford and Skipton stops nearby, and cars can be parked considerably in Cononley, which is 3 miles (4.8 km) south of Skipton.*
Turn left along the road into the village and look for a foot-bridge on your left, just before The Railway inn on your right. Turn left across this and follow the metalled footpath past the sports club to a road. Go left along this for 200 yards (183 m), then turn right up Windle Lane. Go through the entrance to 'Highview' (bed & breakfast) and turn right immediately to cross a stile.

2 *Turn left immediately to climb with a hedge on your left and a wall on your right. Reach a stile, to the left of the gate at the top of the field, and squeeze through. Turn left to follow a path beside the wall on your left. Go ahead over a stone stile in the next corner and maintain your direction to go through a gate ahead. Continue along the clear track to go through a kissing-gate beside a gate.*

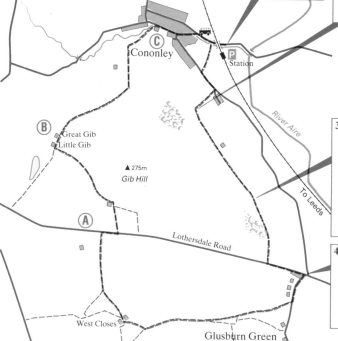

3 *Follow the clear track as it veers slightly uphill to cross a stone stile in the wall on your right. Maintain your direction along this clear path to some trees. Go ahead through a kissing-gate beside a gate to walk with a wall on your left. Go ahead over a stile beside a gate and turn left along a road (Lothersdale Road).*

4 *Turn right up Green Lane and turn right again up Binns Lane. Go ahead past Binns Lane Farm, Green House Farm and Scott House Farm on your left, with the metalled lane deteriorating to a rough track.*

Over

0   1 mile

0   1 km

10 A farm access track comes from the left to join your path. Descend with it and bear right at the bottom to reach Cononley. Turn right along the Main Street to return to the railway station.

9 Go ahead through a gate and walk beside the wall on your left to cross a stile beside a gate. Go on down the path to a gate in the wall on your left. Turn left through it and down a walled track.

8 Bear left across this field towards the left hand side of the left of two houses ('Little Gib'). Cross a wooden stile and turn right to pass the cottage on your left. Go ahead through a gate to pass 'Great Gib'. Continue through a gate to follow a path beside a wall on your left.

7 Cross the road to take the path on the left to Manor Farm. Follow the path past the farmhouse on your left and go through the farmyard to a gate. Follow the track as it bears right. Continue beside a wall on your left, then bear left through a waymarked gateway to cross a waymarked stile in the far corner.

6 Cross the left hand gate in the corner to continue along a rough track beside a wall on your right. Go ahead through a gate and walk with the wall still on your right through another gate. Go ahead over a cattle grid to reach a road and turn right along it.

5 Cross a cattle grid and bear right along a track across the field to West Closes Farm. Turn right to go through a gate between the two farmhouses and cross a paddock to go through another gate. Go ahead with a wall on your right to a gate in the corner of the field. Go through it and veer left towards the far left corner of the next field.

Cononley

Station

River Aire

To Leeds

Ⓒ

Ⓑ Great Gib
Little Gib

▲ 275m
Gib Hill

Ⓐ

Lothersdale Road

West Closes

Glusburn Green

A Gib Hill suggests that this was the site of a gibbet, or gallows. The executed bodies of wrongdoers were then put on display to warn others.

B Lead mines have been worked here since Roman times, if not earlier. Cornish miners were imported in the early 19th century and their chimney and engine house stand restored on private land.

C Cononley has attractive cottages and an amazingly long terrace.

LOTHERSDALE

4 miles (6.4 km) Moderate

0 ————————————————— 1 mile
0 ————————————————— 1 km

A tall mill chimney does not detract from the beauty of Lothersdale. Charlotte Brontë was glad to leave, however, after less than three months, but this was due to her relationship with Mrs Sidgwick (see below). There are fine views of Earl Crag and its monuments to reward your climb up from Leys Beck to Cowling Hill.

1 *Start from The Hare & Hounds in Lothersdale, near which cars can be parked. This is on a minor road about 5 miles (8 km) south of Skipton and 2 miles (3.2 km) west of Cononley, the nearest railway station.*
With your back to the Hare & Hounds, turn left along the road. Ignore a signposted path to Cowling on your right.

2 *Turn left up a signposted path to Tow Top Moor. When the walled path opens out into a diamond-shaped field, go straight ahead. Continue along a walled track in the top corner. Go through a gate ahead to join a track coming from your left. After 100 yards (91 m) turn right over a stile and walk beside the wall on your left. Bear left to a gate.*

3 *Cross the stile beside the gate and turn right along Babyhouse Lane. When you reach a crossroads, turn right along the road to Lothersdale for 150 yards (137 m). Turn left over a stile beside a gate to follow a signposted path. Descend with a wall on your left and reach a stile in the bottom corner near trees. Turn left over it.*

4 *Follow a wall on your right to a stile beside a gate. Turn right over this and turn left immediately to go ahead with a hedge on your left. Continue over a ladder stile in the wall ahead. Follow the wall on your left to a stone stile. Cross it and turn right for a few paces before turning left, through the farmyard of 'Leys House'.*

5 *Turn right down a walled track. Bear left with this track to cross a foot-bridge over a stream (Leys Beck). Continue up an old green lane to reach a metalled lane. Go straight across. Keep climbing to reach Long Lane.*

6 *Turn right along Long Lane. Ignore a farm entrance on your right and a lane on your left. Bear right to Cowling Hill and leave the lane opposite the graveyard of the Baptist church, turning right over a stile.*

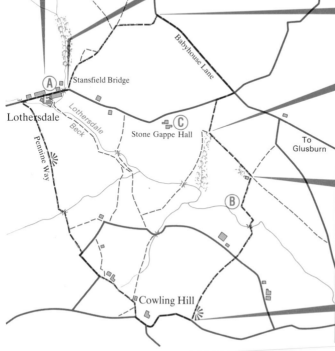

Stansfield Bridge

Lothersdale

Babyhouse Lane

Lothersdale Beck

Pennine Way

Stone Gappe Hall

To Glusburn

Cowling Hill

Over

LOTHERSDALE

Continued

8 *Bear right along the lane to the next corner. Go ahead here over a stile to the right of the gate. From now on your path is very well defined by the tread of countless feet, for this is part of the Pennine Way. Follow a wall on your left, then veer right above the trees and descend to a gate. Continue with a wall on your left, cross a stream (Surgill Beck), go through a gate and walk with a wall on your right. Continue through a gate and past Woodhead Farm on your right. Notice the view across the valley on your right to Stone Gappe.*

9 *Ignore the Alternative Route on your left at the Pennine Way signpost. Go ahead to reach the road and turn right to the start.*

7 *Follow the signposted path to Lothersdale, walking with a wall on your right. When you come to a house, bear left across a stile (covered by a mesh gate) and continue with a wall on your left for 120 yards (110 m). Then follow the path through a gap on your left. Go ahead through a gate and pass farm buildings on your right to reach a lane at a corner.*

A Lothersdale is a charming mixture of picturesque cottages and a textile mill. Quakers used to live here and they built a meeting house in 1776. In 1791 eight local Quakers were imprisoned in York Castle for non-payment of the tithe and the resultant fines. One of these 'Lothersdale Martyrs' died in prison. While this event was putting the place on the map, the old cornmill was converted to a textile mill. Although this was an excellent site for water power, production of cotton and silk increased when a steam engine was first installed in 1842. This was replaced in 1850 and a 90 foot (27 m) chimney built. Water power was still important and the biggest indoor water wheel in England was installed in 1869. Its diameter was 45 feet (13.5 m).

B The flat field on the right alongside the beck is thought to be the site of 'Lothers' camp. Lother is from the old English 'lodre', and means beggar.

C Stone Gappe Hall was where Charlotte Brontë had her first job. She walked here from Haworth in 1839, at the age of 23, to be the governess to the children of John Sidgwick. Charlotte found Mrs Sidgwick devoid of 'every fine feeling' and the five children were 'little devils incarnate'. Stone Gappe became the model for Gateshead Hall in the novel *Jane Eyre*. Delius, the composer, also visited here to see his sister and play for her on her piano.

Walk 3
CARLETON
4.5 miles (7.2 km) Strenuous

Variety is the essence of this walk. It starts and finishes in a pleasant, sturdy village which is dominated by its mill. Stamina is demanded for the long, steady climb up Ramshaw. Take your time and enjoy the delightful heather. The views are extensive and superb. The return path is a real contrast, with streams and wooded glens. Carleton has a truly enviable setting.

1 Start from the church of St Mary the Virgin, Carleton. This village is 2 miles (3.2 km) south-west of Skipton, from where there is a Pennine Motors bus. Cars can be parked considerably in the village centre.
Turn left from the church porch to follow a paved path through kissing-gates to a road at St Mary's Green. Bear left along the road out of the village, but ignore a turning on the left to Skipton. Pass a farm on your left.

2 Go up steps on your right, turn right through a gap stile and follow a path to a farm track. Go ahead across this and over a stile in the fence opposite. Aim just to the left of the trees on the horizon as you climb. Cross a stile in the top wall, to the left of the gate in the corner. Veer to the left across the next field to cross a stile in the wall ahead. Turn right along a track.

3 Veer left with the track towards trees. Go through a gateway as the track bends left to a farmhouse, but turn right immediately over a stile. Walk with a wall on your left to pass through a gate. Go ahead to a stile and climb with a wall on your left to cross another stile ahead.

4 You now face a steep climb up Ramshaw. This high, broad ridge offers excellent views across Airedale over the wall on your left. Reach a stile in a corner and cross it to walk with the wall now on your right.

5 Go ahead over a stile in the next corner to walk with a wall on your left again. Go over another stile and bear right along the clear track from a gate on your left.

6 Join another track to continue with a wall on your left. Go through a gate which leads onto a lane and turn right. Go ahead past a road turning on your left, then past a plantation of conifer trees on your right. Turn right at the next road junction.

Over

0   1 mile

0   1 km

10 *Go down the field to cross a stile in the wall ahead, near its right corner. Continue parallel to another stream on your right. Notice where a hedge comes in to the opposite side of the stream. Veer right here to step across the stream where a stile faces you on the other side. Bear left after crossing this, along a waymarked path and look for a gate in the right hand hedge near the bottom of the field. Turn right through it and cross a field to go through a gate. Go ahead along a track.*

9 *Descend towards trees on your right, go past the remains of an old wall and follow a narrow path ahead for 350 yards (310 m) down to stepping stones across a stream. These are just after a fence on the opposite side. Go up a path with the stream now on your left. Go through a gate in the fence ahead.*

8 *Reach the bottom corner of the field and ignore a gate on your left to go through a gate ahead. Walk with a wall on your right and go through a gate to the right of a farmhouse. Turn right over a stile in the wall to walk down a field parallel to a wall on your left. Go ahead over a stile.*

11 *Follow this track back to Carleton, crossing a bridge and following The Wend to a road. Turn right to pass The Swan and turn left. Turn right just before the Post Office to return to the church.*

Church

Carleton

Park Lane

Ramshaw

Burnt Hill

7 *Go down the road for 200 yards (183 m), then turn left, opposite where the trees end on your right. Descend with a wall on your left.*

A Ramshaw's high ridge, a northern outpost of the South Pennines which provides a fine view across Airedale to the Yorkshire Dales, shelters Carleton from easterly winds. Ramshaw's church is Victorian, but there are 17th-century almshouses at the eastern end of the village. These have a courtyard hemmed in by spinning galleries. Today, carpets are made at the mill.

B Sturdily built dry-stone walls are a feature of this Millstone grit landscape. Some stiles are formed by steps in these walls, while others are narrow gaps. Look along the wall to the left of the stile at walk direction **10** to see an example of a creep hole. Also known as a cripple hole, this allows sheep but not cattle to pass from field to field.

Walk 4
THE FOREST OF TRAWDEN
5.3 miles (8.5 km) Moderate

0   1 mile
0   1 km

You won't find many trees in the Forest of Trawden today, but the rich peat testifies to their former presence. Saxons used to hunt in the forest, which was gradually felled for clear farmland. Lime was added to the soil to improve it and stone walls were built to enclose it. This walk crosses 'unimproved' moorland which rises to form Boulsworth Hill to the south of the waymarked Pendle Way.

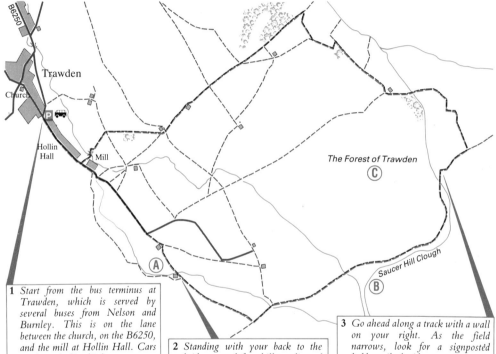

1 *Start from the bus terminus at Trawden, which is served by several buses from Nelson and Burnley. This is on the lane between the church, on the B6250, and the mill at Hollin Hall. Cars can be parked in this lane.*
Go up the lane to pass the mill on your left. Continue over a bridge and ahead to a bend on your left. Leave the lane here to go ahead along a farm track. Go past farm buildings on your right and continue through a gate. Walk with a wall on your right to go through a second gate. Continue ahead along a track to cross a beck and divert to the right to see Lumb Spout waterfall. Return to the bridge.

2 *Standing with your back to the bridge, veer left uphill, as directed by a waymark post. Cross a stile beside a gate in the corner of a wall and continue with a wall on your right. Go ahead over a ladder stile and turn left along a track with a wall now on your left. This is part of the Pendle Way, so follow the 'witch' waymarks. Your path runs above a stream on your right. Eventually descend to cross this stream where indicated by a waymark. Bear left to cross a gap stile beside a gate.*

3 *Go ahead along a track with a wall on your right. As the field narrows, look for a signposted ladder stile beside a gate on your left and turn left over it. Follow a fence, then a wall, on your left to cross a stile beside a gate. Bear left to pass Dean House on your right, then go left across a step stile in a wall and bear right down to cross a stile in a fence before a stream. Cross the stream and a stile in the fence on the other side, then veer right uphill to a waymark post. Turn right through a gap stile near the top of the wall on your right and go ahead to a stile on your left.*

Over

0   1 mile

0   1 km

6 *Go ahead over a stile keeping the wall on your left. Continue over two more stiles and pass a farmhouse on your left before going over a stile in the corner of a field. Pass a farmhouse on your right and turn right over a stile beside a gate. Turn left along a waymarked path with a wall on your left. Go ahead through a gap stile and down the left hand side of a field, passing trees on your left. Turn left through a tiny gate to bear left down a track. Cross a bridge over a beck to the right of the mill. Turn right along the lane back to the bus terminus in Trawden, or your parked car.*

5 *Go through a gate towards the house and turn left up a waymarked path to the top gate. Bear right along a path which climbs gradually to cross a stile beside a gate. Bear right down the metalled track. When you are level with a wall on your left, look for a waymarked path and turn sharply left to follow it with the wall now on your right. Continue over a stile with trees now on your left. When the wall on your right goes right, continue ahead through trees. Soon there is a wall on your left. Go over a stile in the corner and proceed ahead with a wall on your left.*

4 *Cross the stile in the wall on your left at Bank House and turn right as waymarked to go through a gate. Follow the track above a wall on your right. You soon pass trees behind a fence on your left, then go ahead over a stile in a corner to continue beside the wall on your right for 30 yards (27 m). Turn right to cross the wall and reach the corner of a field on the other side. Bear left towards Copy House and follow a path between a fenced plantation of trees on your left and a wall on your right.*

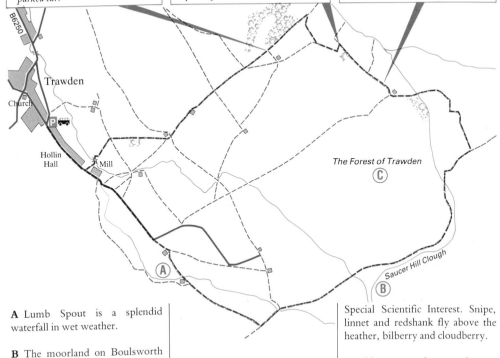

Trawden

Church

Hollin Hall

Mill

The Forest of Trawden

Ⓒ

Ⓐ

Ⓑ

Saucer Hill Clough

A Lumb Spout is a splendid waterfall in wet weather.

B The moorland on Boulsworth Hill has been designated as a Site of

Special Scientific Interest. Snipe, linnet and redshank fly above the heather, bilberry and cloudberry.

C Alder trees used to grow here.

Walk 5

PINHAW BEACON

3 miles (4.8 km) Easy

This walk leads to one of the finest viewpoints of the South Pennines. Pinhaw Beacon is 1273 ft (388 m) high, but you can park in a lay-by at an altitude of about 1130 ft (340 m), and enjoy the view without having to make a strenuous climb. Although only of modest height, Pinhaw Beacon is the highest point within a wide area, offering great reward for little effort.

1 *Start from the lay-by on the high road between Colne and Skipton that crosses Elslack Moor. The lay-by is close to a cattle grid near a junction with a lane down to Elslack. This is about 5 miles (8 km) north-east of Colne and 5 miles (8 km) south-west of Skipton.From the lay-by, turn right to the road junction and go left up the signposted Pennine Way with a wall on your right.*

To Skipton

To Elslack

Ransable Hill

Elslack Moor

388m

B

Pinhaw Beacon

To Colne

P

6 *Go over a stile ahead to reach the road and turn left along it, across a cattle grid. Walk with the trees and the view on your right back to the lay-by.*

5 *Turn left and leave the Pennine Way to turn left again over another stile. Go ahead with a wall on your left. Eventually, descend to the road.*

4 *Continue along the Pennine Way, to reach a wall on your right. Follow this wall down and around to the right to cross a stile into a field.*

2 *Follow the Pennine Way as it bears left, away from the wall, to reach Ordnance Survey column S4451 on top of Pinhaw Beacon.*

3 *Follow the well trodden path of the Pennine Way. After about 250 yards (229 m) there is an unofficial path on your left to the Beacon.*

A Pinhaw Beacon is a large grassy mound surmounted by an Ordnance Survey triangulation point and surrounded by a sea of heather. At 1273 ft (388 m) it is the highest point north of the A6068 road between Colne and Cross Hills and south of the Yorkshire Dales. It has, therefore, an all-round view. Looking north, you can see Pendle Hill on your left, then, sweeping right, Ingleborough, Pen-y-ghent and the limestone hills of Malham. Skipton is the town down on your right.

B In the early 1800s Pinhaw Beacon was attended by Beacon Guards. Two at a time came from each of the nearby villages of Elslack, Carleton and Lothersdale to live in a little hut for a week. One of the Beacon Guards from Elslack was found dead in the snow just 150 yards (137 m) from the hut one severe winter, when he had tried to return from the village with provisions. His name was Robert Wilson and a low stone monument marks the spot where he died on 29th January, 1805, aged 59 years.

Walk 6
WYCOLLER
2.3 miles (3.7 km) Moderate

Ancient bridges and vaccary walling (medieval rows of upright stones) can be seen around Wycoller, a hamlet which survives as a reminder of the days before the Industrial Revolution. It has fine scenery, but is most famous for its literary associations. Ruins here are evocative of the feelings which moved Charlotte Brontë when she wrote 'Jane Eyre'.

2 Turn left across the packhorse bridge to visit the ruins of the Hall, then climb the steps behind the ruins. Go ahead through a stile beside a gate and up an avenue with vaccary walling on your left and trees behind a fence on your right.

4 Go ahead to cross a stile and veer left uphill to a gap in the next wall. Follow the distinct path across the next field to a ladder stile and go on to another ladder stile. Cut across the bottom of the next field to cross a waymarked gap stile.

Wycoller · Wycoller Hall · Wycoller Country Park · Clapper Bridge

1 Start from the car park at the entrance to the hamlet of Wycoller, which is easily reached from Colne via the A6068 to Keighley and the B6250 to Trawden. A Lancashire County Council Leisure Link bus (no 80) comes here from Burnley, Nelson and Colne on Sundays and Bank Holidays between Good Friday and 1st October.
Walk along the footpath into the hamlet.

3 Notice a ladder stile beside a gate on your left. Turn RIGHT here to follow a waymarked path across a field and through a gateway to the next.

5 Join a track to pass a bungalow on your left, then pass a house on the left and go through a waymarked gate in a corner. Turn left to climb a ladder stile beside a gate and bear right diagonally downhill to pass through a small gate leading to a foot-bridge over a beck. Cross it and turn right along the clear track which is part of both the Brontë Way and the Pendle Way. Follow this back to Wycoller.

A The packhorse bridge has had its stones worn down by the tread of countless feet. Just upstream is the clapper bridge. The word clapper refers to the sound of clogs worn by the weavers who used this bridge. They washed their cloth in the stream and used the bridge to reach Tenter Field on the slopes above the Hall, where the cloth was stretched to dry on tenterhooks.

B Wycoller Hall is ruined now, but still retains its dignity. Signs of decay would have been apparent in Brontë times. The hall was in its heyday around 1600, when Wycoller was a thriving handloom weaving centre. It was brought to rack and ruin by the Cunliffe family, the last of whom died at Wycoller in 1818 and whose grandmother had remarried to become Elizabeth Eyre. Her son by this marriage, Thomas Eyre, would have been eligible to inherit the hall following Cunliffe's death if he had renounced the Roman Catholic faith. This he refused to do. No doubt he inspired the name 'Jane Eyre'. This novel was written by Charlotte Brontë in 1847, when 'Even when within a very short distance of the manor house you could see nothing of it, so thick and dark grew the timber of the gloomy wood about it. Iron gates between granite pillars showed me where to enter, and passing through them, I found myself at once in the twilight of close-ranked trees. There was a grass grown track descending the forest aisle between hoar and knotty shafts and under branched arches'. Charlotte Brontë called it Ferndean Manor, and you can still see the old fireplace where the blind Rochester supported his head 'against the high, old-fashioned mantelpiece'.

C Vacarry walls were erected to enclose cattle-rearing farms.

D This is Clam Bridge, formed by a great slab of gritstone. Washed away recently in a flash flood, it is being reinstated.

Walk 7

PENDLE HILL

5 miles (8 km) Strenuous

Scale: 0 — 1 mile / 0 — 1 km

Come on a fine day to enjoy some marvellous views from an ancient beacon site. Pen is the old Celtic word for a top, while Penhille was the original English name for this harsh, rugged, Millstone grit feature, covered with bracken, heather and cotton grass.

5 *Pass Pendle House Farm and turn left to follow the wall on your left downhill to a gate. Veer right across the next field and go over a stile to pass Brown House Farm. Follow the path near the stream down to a lane. Turn left to reach a foot-bridge on your right, which you cross to walk with the stream on your left back to Barley. Turn right along the lane to the bus turnaround.*

1 *Start from the Information Centre at the picnic site and car park in Barley. This village is about 3 miles (4.8 km) north-west of Nelson. There is an infrequent bus service (no 205) from Nelson and Clitheroe.*
Walk through the picnic site and past the children's playground to cross Barley Water to the bus turnaround. Go left along the road, then turn right up a lane to Barley Green.

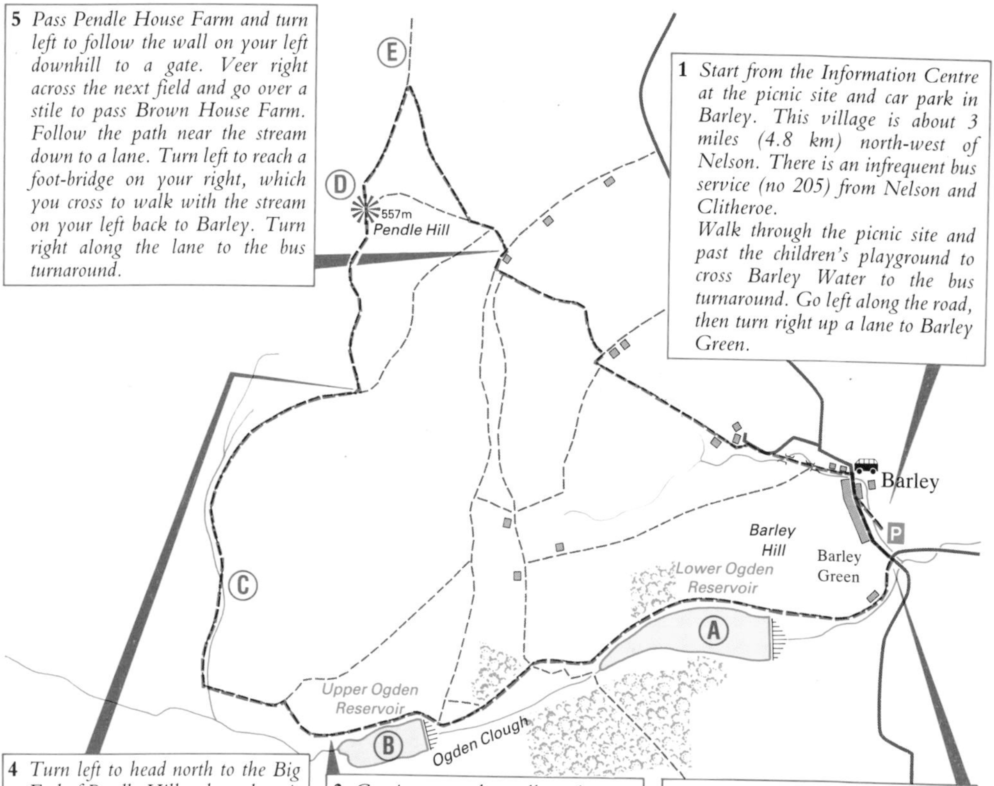

Map labels: E, D, 557m Pendle Hill, C, B, A, Barley, Barley Hill, Barley Green, Lower Ogden Reservoir, Upper Ogden Reservoir, Ogden Clough, P

4 *Turn left to head north to the Big End of Pendle Hill, where there is an Ordnance Survey triangulation point. After admiring the view, continue in the same direction to reach a wall. An unofficial path goes ahead here down to Robin Hood's Well, but the Pendle Way, which this walk follows, turns sharply right to descend along a well maintained, if steep, path. At the bottom, turn right.*

3 *Continue up the valley along a path above a stream on your left. Go ahead over a stile and follow a path which continues above the stream on your left to a waymark post. This indicates where you turn right uphill, on the left hand side of the stream at Boar Clough. The route is cairned and re-crosses the stream. Go right at a fork and keep to the line of cairns until a large cairn is reached.*

2 *Although a metalled lane, this is signposted as a bridlepath to Ogden Clough. Follow it to pass a reservoir on your left. Go ahead over a stile beside a gate and pass a Pendle Way signpost on your left. Continue over a stile past a wood on your right. Leave the track when it bears right, going ahead beside the wall instead. Go past a second reservoir on your left.*

Over

PENDLE HILL

Continued

Pendle Hill

A Lower Ogden Reservoir was completed in 1914 and has a capacity of 157 million gallons (714 million litres). Like the earlier Upper Ogden Reservoir, it was built to provide the town of Nelson with drinking water.

B Upper Ogden Reservoir holds 54 million gallons (246 million litres) and was completed in 1906.

C This is Boar Clough. A clough is a gully formed by a stream.

D Pendle Hill is 1831 feet (558 m) high, but its isolation makes it more impressive. Come on a fine day to see Snowdonia, Blackpool Tower, the Lake District peaks, Ingleborough, Whernside and, further east, Pen-y-ghent. Bonfires have been lit here, probably since the Bronze Age. This is where George Fox had a vision that inspired him to found the Quakers, the Society of Friends. It is also associated with witches, and many come here on Hallowe'en.

E Robin Hood's Well is an ancient holy well which George Fox said had the best water in Lancashire when he drank from it on Good Friday, 1652.

HEBDEN WATER

6 miles (9.7 km) Moderate

0   1 mile
0   1 km

Two wooded valleys are included on this walk from Hebden Bridge, the unofficial capital of the South Pennines. The railway station, bus services, car parks, pubs, restaurants and prize winning Tourist Information Centre make it an ideal touring centre. This route can be linked with Walk 10.

4 *Turn left down steps by a National Trust sign and follow a woodland path upstream to Gibson Mill, keeping the river on your left.*

3 *Pass a farmhouse on your right and take a walled lane above the farm for 100 yards (91 m), then turn sharply left and then right to go up a stone staircase. This leads to a lane where you turn right, with trees on your left. After 200 yards (183 m), bear right down the route of the Calderdale Way, a lane which leads to New Bridge. Go across the bridge on your right.*

2 *Turn right at the end of the lane, then left to re-cross the river. Follow the lane to the left past swings. Shortly after the lane veers right, a path off to the left leads to a foot-bridge. Cross it, and cross a stile. Climb a steep lane ahead to a junction where you turn right to follow a lane past houses. Take a woodland path ahead and bear right downhill at a fork. Bear left when you reach a track coming from the bowling green. Bear left at the next junction to gradually ascend.*

Hebden Water

Hebden Dale

New Bridge

Midgehole

Lumb Mills

A6033

Nutclough

Mytholm

Hebden Bridge

A646

1 *Start from the Information Centre in Hebden Bridge, beside which is a car park. Bus stops are nearby, and there are frequent services to the railway station from Leeds, Manchester and Preston. The Information Centre is on the A646 (Burnley to Halifax road) near where it crosses a bridge in the middle of the town.*
From the rear of the car park, walk upstream along the riverside path. Cross the pack horse bridge and shortly turn right into Hangingroyd Lane.

Over

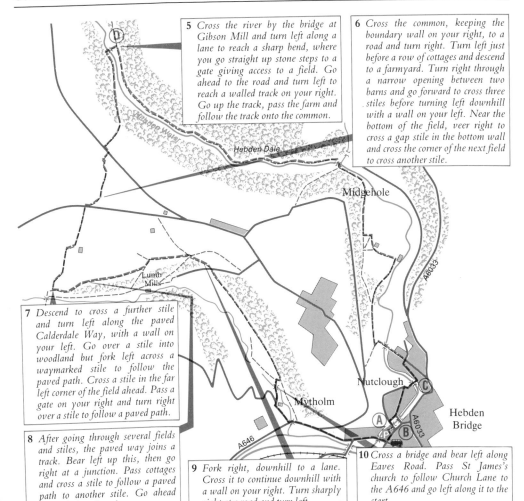

5 Cross the river by the bridge at Gibson Mill and turn left along a lane to reach a sharp bend, where you go straight up stone steps to a gate giving access to a field. Go ahead to the road and turn left to reach a walled track on your right. Go up the track, pass the farm and follow the track onto the common.

6 Cross the common, keeping the boundary wall on your right, to a road and turn right. Turn left just before a row of cottages and descend to a farmyard. Turn right through a narrow opening between two barns and go forward to cross three stiles before turning left downhill with a wall on your left. Near the bottom of the field, veer right to cross a gap stile in the bottom wall and cross the corner of the next field to cross another stile.

7 Descend to cross a further stile and turn left along the paved Calderdale Way, with a wall on your left. Go over a stile into woodland but fork left across a waymarked stile to follow the paved path. Cross a stile in the far left corner of the field ahead. Pass a gate on your right and turn right over a stile to follow a paved path.

8 After going through several fields and stiles, the paved way joins a track. Bear left up this, then go right at a junction. Pass cottages and cross a stile to follow a paved path to another stile. Go ahead along the broad track.

9 Fork right, downhill to a lane. Cross it to continue downhill with a wall on your right. Turn sharply right at a road and turn left.

10 Cross a bridge and bear left along Eaves Road. Pass St James's church to follow Church Lane to the A646 and go left along it to the start.

A This old packhorse bridge dates from the early 16th century, when it replaced an earlier wooden bridge.

B St George's Square is actually a triangle. On a Good Friday you may see the traditional Pace Egg Play, in which mummers perform the victory of Good (represented by King George) over Evil (the Black Prince).

C Nutclough Mill was a highly successful co-operative mill between 1873 and 1919.

D Gibson Mill (see Walk 10 for full details).

Walk 9

STOODLEY PIKE MONUMENT

6 miles (9.7 km) Strenuous

The monument at Stoodley Pike is a popular destination for ramblers from Hebden Bridge or Todmorden. It stands at 1310 feet (399 m) above sea level and provides fine views on a clear day, but it can also be a cold, windy spot, as befits a major feature on the wild, bleak Pennine Way. This route can be linked with Walk **11**.

A Before leaving Hebden Bridge, look behind and up at the Victorian 'double-decker' housing.

B The present Stoodley Pike monument was erected in 1856, but it had a predecessor, built to mark the surrender of Paris in 1814. As a monument to peace it was started just a year too soon, as Napoleon escaped from Elba while it was still under construction. The monument was completed in 1815, the year of Waterloo. Curiously, it collapsed on the afternoon that the Russian ambassador left London before the declaration of the Crimean War on 8th February, 1854. The present monument was built to replace it in the year of the Peace. It stands 120 feet (37 m) high and there are steps inside it leading to a viewing gallery. The view is well worth the dark (and cold) trip up the stairs. To the south can be seen Holme Moss, while Boulsworth Hill stands to the north. Todmorden lies at your feet, to the west.

Stoodley Pike Monument

Over

0   1 mile

0   1 km

Hebden
Bridge

1 Start from the Information Centre in Hebden Bridge, which is easily reached by train or bus. There is a car park beside the Tourist Information Centre.
Bear right over the bridge at West End to follow Market Street as far as the third turning on your left, which is Hebble End. Go left here to cross the river and the canal, then bear right for 0.5 mile (0.8 km) up Horsehold Road. Keep straight ahead along a grassy track when the road turns left to Horsehold.

2 Walk with trees on your right. Ignore a path on your left and continue with a small stream on your right to a stile ahead which leads to an old green lane. Turn right along this and bend left, then right with this walled track. Go ahead with a wall on your left.

3 Reach a junction with another track and turn left up it. Pass a farm on your left, then turn right along another track which takes you past Swillington Farm on your right. Go through the gate to follow a wall to a corner, then turn left across moorland. This is the well trodden Pennine Way.

7 Bear left at a junction above a wall. Follow the path down to a road. Turn left to bear right over a railway bridge, then go left briefly. Turn right by the first house onto a path which descends to the canal towpath. Turn right along the towpath to the lock. Cross the canal and follow the surfaced path down the slope to the road end near the post office and school. Walk along this road back to the Information Centre.

6 At the junction, turn right along a track. Bear left downhill when you reach a track signposted to Old Chamber. At a corner where the track bends right, keep straight ahead along a grassy walled lane. This takes a tunnel under another lane and continues down through woodland, where it bears left to a fence, then goes right.

5 Bear left into a broad, walled track (Dicks Lane). When you reach a ruined barn, bear left downhill parallel to a wall on your left. Ignore the track on your left to continue with the wall on your left and moorland on your right. Go left at the next turning to take a walled track past Rake Head Farm. Descend to a junction.

4 Go over a ladder stile and immediately turn right to cross another stile. Go ahead to Stoodley Pike Monument. Retrace your steps to cross the last stile and then continue ahead with the wall on your left to the corner.

Station

A646

A646

Kershaw Farm

Swillington
Farm

Ⓑ
Stoodley Pike
Monument

23

HARDCASTLE CRAGS

2.5 miles (4 km) Easy

0 _____ 1 mile

0 _____ 1 km

This woodland walk is a delight in any season, although the autumn tints can lend a stunning touch of colour. A telling compliment is the fact that this valley was for many years the place where Swiss immigrants to England used to gather for their annual meeting, since the valley is so reminiscent of their native land. This route can be linked with Walk 8.

5 Walk back to the bridge to Gibson Mill with the river on your left and a reservoir on your right. Go right away from it, then fork right along the upper track, with a wall on your left. Turn sharply right up a track which joins a more level track to continue to the car park.

1 Start from the National Trust's car park for Hardcastle Crags at Clough Hole, on your right as you drive north along the lane from Heptonstall to Nelson.
From the notice board at the bottom of the car park, go ahead along the path down to Gibson Mill.

4 Turn left at another green topped post to follow the path to a foot-bridge. Cross this and go left along a riverside path. Cross a small foot-bridge over a tributary which crosses your path and bear right uphill along a narrow woodland path (this is **before** a foot-bridge crosses the river on your left). At a junction with a broad woodland path, bear left, above the river. This gradually descends to a fence on your right and bears left to the river.

3 Fork left off the track at a green topped post and go through a gate to follow a downhill path.

2 Having crossed the river at the mill, turn left along a track to walk above the river on your left.

A This is Gibson Mill, founded by Abraham Gibson around 1800 as a water-powered cotton spinning mill. The poor soil and wet climate of the Pennines encouraged people to spin and weave cloth for a living, rather than grow crops. A thriving medieval cottage industry, which led to the building of the local packhorse bridges, was transformed by inventions which mechanised weaving, such as Hargreaves' 'Spinning Jenny' and John Kay's 'flying shuttle'. Then Arkwright's 'water frame' caused the textile industry to move from the cottages to mills which used water power. At first these were situated in the remote valleys where the water flowed faster. They were also devoted mainly to spinning, with weaving still done by handloom weavers. The advent of steam soon brought even more dramatic changes. The chimney of Gibson Mill was added when steam power was introduced in the 1860s (thus overcoming the loss of water in dry, frosty weather). Children aged from 10 to 12 worked a 72 hour week here for half a crown (12½p). It closed in the 1890s as a result of competition from Calderdale's larger and less remote mills. The community's reluctance to lose the mill led to it being used as a dance hall and a roller skating rink during this century.

B This deep valley is a legacy of the last ice age, aided by the ever rushing torrent of Hebden Water. The Crags are stacks of Millstone grit formed by erosion. They are partially concealed by trees which were planted in the late 19th century. These include the native deciduous species such as oak, birch, beech, ash and rowan. Such woodland provides habitat for a wide range of plants and wildlife.

WITHENS CLOUGH RESERVOIR

4.3 miles (6.9 km) Moderate, boggy in places

0 _____ 1 mile

0 _____ 1 km

This is a moorland walk, with the bonus of a reservoir and a conifer plantation. The section along the Pennine Way up to Stoodley Pike Monument has a splendid view over Todmorden on your left. The Te Deum stone adds to the wayfaring atmosphere. Do remember to dress appropriately, since there is a small boggy patch before one gate. This route can be linked with Walk 9.

4 DO NOT go ahead along a walled path facing you. Instead turn right as waymarked. Walk with the wall on your left uphill to a gate in the corner on your left. Near this is the Te Deum stone. Cross the stile beside the gate and go ahead. Paving stones soon reappear

5 Reach a signpost and turn right along the edge which is part of the Pennine Way. Bear right at Stoodley Pike Monument to follow the well-defined path to a stile in the wall ahead. Carry on with the wall on your left. Ignore the green lane going left from the corner and go ahead over a stile in the wall facing you.

6 Walk between conifer trees to a gate in the fence ahead. Continue to a stile in the next fence and veer left to a gate, picking your way through a boggy patch. Turn left up a walled track. Pass a ruined farm and proceed to a T junction. Turn right, soon passing a farmhouse on your left. At the bend by the next farm, turn right with the track downhill back to the car park.

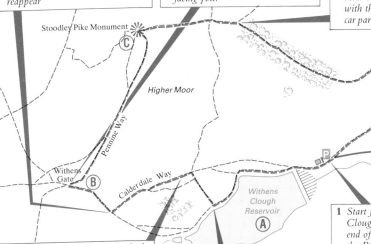

3 Walk with a wall on your right for three fields, then turn right through a gap stile to turn left immediately along a paved and waymarked part of the Calderdale Way, with the wall on your left. Go ahead across an open field to a waymark post. Continue until you reach a wall facing you.

2 Look out for a Calderdale Way post on your right where you turn right up the uphill path. Reach a corner of a wall ahead and continue uphill with a wall on your left. Turn left as waymarked along a section of the Calderdale Way.

1 Start from the car park at Withens Clough Reservoir. This is at the end of a lane which goes west from the B6138 at Cragg Vale, 2 miles (3.2 km) south of Mytholmroyd. You can also use the minibus service up Cragg Vale.
Go up the path that is waymarked with the emblem of the Calderdale Way (a 'c' above a 'w') through the gate towards the reservoir. Walk past the water on your left.

A Withens Clough Reservoir was built to supply Morley with water.

B The Te Deum stone is a sacred mark at the summit of the ancient packhorse track between Crag and Mankinholes. Look for the inscription 'TE DEUM LAUDAMUS' – 'We praise thee O Lord!'

C Stoodley Pike Monument (see Walk 9 for details).

LUMB MILL

5 miles (8 km) Moderate

0   1 mile

0   1 km

A peaceful stroll beside a canal is followed by a more taxing walk along part of the Pennine Way. This leads to a delightful wooded clough at Colden Water, which is followed back to Hebden Bridge. Those interested in industrial archaeology will be in their element here, as the path goes past ruins of old mills.

4 *Bear right on a wider track and bend left into a steep, walled path uphill to a gate on your left. Turn right here to follow a walled track. Pass a turning to a farmhouse on your right, then turn left up a narrow, waymarked path to a stile. Go ahead with a wall on your left.*

6 *Fork right to follow the tops of retaining walls of small dams always keeping the stream to your right. Cross the stream at Lumb Mill and now walk with the stream on your left. Go ahead along a track which leads to Church Lane. Bear left along the A646. Station Road is on your right.*

1 *Start from British Rail's station at Hebden Bridge – this is well served by buses, and you can park here. Follow Station Road across a bridge over the River Calder. Just before you come to a bridge over a canal, turn left into the park and walk along the right hand edge of the park to the canal lock level with the centre of Hebden Bridge. Drop onto the towpath and proceed along it with the canal on your left. When the canal is crossed by the Pennine Way (waymarked with an acorn), turn right to cross a bridge over the river and reach the road at a bus stop.*

Colden Water   C   Lumb Mill

Pennine Way

5 *Continue to a road and go ahead over a stile on the other side. Walk with the wall on your left, descending to a narrow, walled path. Cross a track and go down steps to cross Colden Water by the foot-bridge. Turn right and fork right leaving the Pennine Way to keep to a path above the stream on your right. Go ahead through woodland.*

Mytholm

Church

A646

Hebden Bridge

R Calder   B

A

2 *Go right briefly, then turn left up a track (Underbank Avenue). This leads under the railway. Climb the steep, paved and walled path ahead. Pass a house on your left and bear left to reach the ruin and graveyard of Mt Olive Baptist church.*

3 *Notice the Pennine Way sign by the gate and go right for just a few yards, then turn left above the ruined church. Climb to see Stoodley Pike on your left.*

A This section of the Leeds and Manchester Railway was opened in 1840. It was engineered by George Stephenson.

B The Rochdale Canal, which ran from Manchester to Sowerby Bridge opened in 1804, and closed in 1952. This section has been restored.

C The ruins of the 19th-century Lumb Mill stand in the delightfully named Jumble Hole Clough.

HAWKS CLOUGH

3 miles (4.8 km) Easy

The Calder Valley starts to open out east of Hebden Bridge. Good paths in the shade of trees afford views that soon become compulsive. The industrial valley floor is visited at the old hamlet of Hawks Clough, and a relaxing return journey is made beside a canal.

1 *Start from British Rail's station at Hebden Bridge, where you may park your car. This is well served by buses. Go right from the entrance to where metal posts block the access for motorists and turn right under the railway bridge. Take the uphill path ahead at a junction and turn right immediately to pass behind houses. Follow a grassy track uphill with woodland on your left.*

2 *Turn left at the path junction and climb gradually uphill. Reach Wood Top Farm and bear right for about 50 yards (46 m), then turn left along a track. This goes past several buildings.*

3 *The track becomes metalled at 'Park Cottage'. Turn left just after it, going through a small wooden gate. Descend with a wall on your left. Cross a stile in a corner and go ahead over a field to Great Stubb.*

4 *Go ahead to an enclosed area and take the gap to the right of a low outbuilding. A paved path leads to a foot-bridge over the railway. Go across this and follow a hedged path to Caldene Avenue.*

5 *Go right along the road for 50 yards (46 m) and bear left down steps. Go right to a cobbled path and cross the bridge on your left. Cross the main road at a bus stop and turn right for 100 yards (91 m).*

6 *Turn left to a bridge over the canal. Turn right down the steps before it and turn left along the towpath to walk with the canal on your right. Go under the bridge and pass Broadbottom Lock (no 7) on your right. Continue across a road bridge. Pass Mayroyd Mill Lock (no 8).*

7 *Veer left before the next bridge to go up a ramp to Station Road and turn left along it back to the British Rail station.*

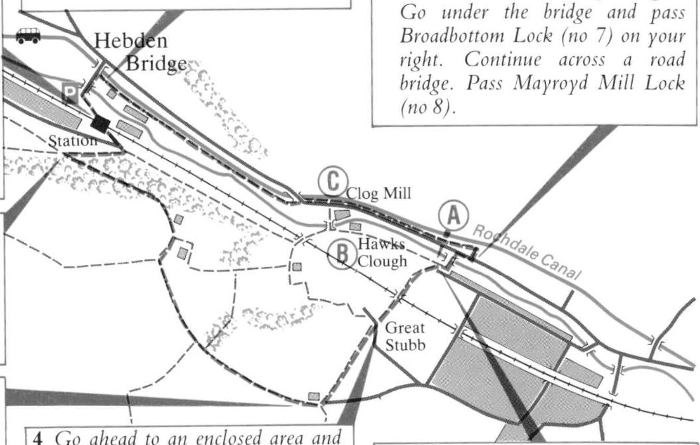

Map labels: Hebden Bridge, Station, Clog Mill, Hawks Clough, Great Stubb, Rochdale Canal, C, A, B

A Hawks Clough lies in the valley of the hawks. One of Calderdale's earliest industrial settlements, it is known to have been the site of a fulling mill in 1310. Today it is a part of Mytholmroyd, but it still has the feel of an independent hamlet. The most recent mill was demolished in the 1970s to provide the grassy area between the canal and the road as you turn back towards Hebden Bridge. Broadbottom Lock has been lovingly restored.

B Here stands the only remaining clog sole mill in Britain. This four storey mill has been a home of clog production for over a century. After a big slump in the demand for clogs, they are now sold as items of fashion as well as for safety in factories. There is a mill shop, and factory tours are a regular feature.

C The road used to cross the canal by a switchback bridge. The opportunity was taken to replace this with a straight section of road in the 1960s, when the canal was disused. The reopening of the Rochdale Canal here was made possible by the building of a tunnel in 1986.

Walk 14
HAWORTH
4.3 miles (6.9 km) Moderate

0 _____ 1 mile
0 _____ 1 km

Haworth is world famous for its connections with the Brontës, so don't expect to escape the crowds on this walk. Allow plenty of time, too, to visit the museum that was once the home of the family, as well as the other places of local interest. The views are breathtaking. This route can be linked with Walk 15.

1 *Start from the Tourist Information Centre in Haworth. This is in the old part of the village on the hill overlooking the railway station. The most exciting way to come here is by steam train on the Keighley and Worth Valley Railway, which links with British Rail at Keighley. There are also bus services, and motorists will find Haworth on the B6142, 4 miles (6.4 km) south of Keighley. There is a car park signposted near the start of this walk.*
Walk to the church (St Michael's) and turn right to pass it on your left. The Brontë Parsonage Museum is soon reached on your left.

3 *Climb with a wall on your left. Go ahead past a farmhouse on your right and up a walled lane to return to the road at another bus stop. Pass this on your right as you follow the road through Stanbury. Reach the bus turnaround and fork left along a lane which is signposted as the path to 'Top Withens, Brontë Waterfalls and Upper Heights'. Ignore a turning on your right, but turn left over the stile beside a gate 75 yards (69 m) after it, opposite a farmhouse. Go ahead with a wall on your left at first, then across a stile in the wooden fence below. Go down the hill to cross another stile in the bottom wall.*

2 *Go ahead past the museum and along a signposted, walled path. Pass houses on your right and continue through a gap stile. Go ahead along a paved path to a road, where you bear left. Fork left up Cemetery Road and go ahead to a lay-by on your right where there is a fine view across Sladenbeck, towards the Worth Valley. Veer right down the track towards the reservoir but stop at a gate and turn right down a footpath to the road, keeping a wall on your left. Turn left along the road. When you reach a bus stop, turn right to pass cottages on your left. Turn left over the stile before a gate.*

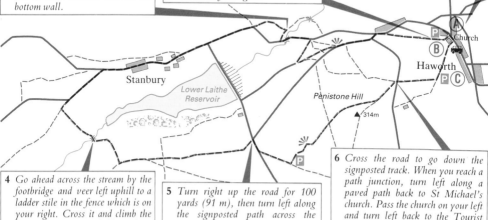

Stanbury

Lower Laithe
Reservoir

Penistone Hill

▲ 314m

Haworth

P Ⓐ Church
Ⓑ
P Ⓒ

4 *Go ahead across the stream by the footbridge and veer left uphill to a ladder stile in the fence which is on your right. Cross it and climb the steep hill to another ladder stile in the top left hand corner of this field. Cross this and turn left to follow a track past the ruins of a farmhouse on your left. Follow the track to a road.*

5 *Turn right up the road for 100 yards (91 m), then turn left along the signposted path across the moorland of Penistone Hill Country Park. You can wander at will over this moor, but this route is waymarked and leads to a road opposite the signposted track back to Haworth.*

6 *Cross the road to go down the signposted track. When you reach a path junction, turn left along a paved path back to St Michael's church. Pass the church on your left and turn left back to the Tourist Information Centre.*

Over

A This parish church is much altered from the one that the Rev. Patrick Brontë knew. His successor, the Rev. John Wade, virtually rebuilt it in the Victorian mania for restoration. Look for the Brontë vault inside the church, near the family pew. Two devoted Brontë servants, Tabitha Aykroyd and Martha Brown, are buried in the churchyard.

B The parsonage that was once the home of the Brontës is now a museum in the care of the Brontë Society. It is open every day of the year, except from 24th to 26th December and the last full week in January and the first two weeks of February, 11 - 5.30 (4.30 in winter). Patrick Brontë hailed from Emdale, in Ireland and was born in 1777. His original name was Brunty (or Prunty). An evangelical anglican vicar spotted his scholastic talent and helped him get to Cambridge in 1802, where he soon changed his name to Brontë, after the Italian title of Lord Nelson, also Duke of Brontë. Patrick graduated and was ordained in 1806. He came to Yorkshire and finally settled in Haworth with his wife and six young children in April 1820. Within 18 months his wife, Maria, had died of cancer. Her last words were 'Oh, God, my poor children – oh, God, my poor children.'

The eldest child, also called Maria, was just seven. Elizabeth Branwell, Patrick's sister-in-law, came from Cornwall to bring up the children. She resented her

The Brontë Parsonage, Haworth

situation and hated Yorkshire, but her stern sense of religious duty made her respond nobly to the task. Her severe discipline pervaded the household, which was run with military precision. Some saw the parsonage as a cold and cheerless place, but, while working as a governess in York, Anne remembered it as a place of joy. She wrote:

'Restore to me that little spot,
With grey walls compassed round.
Oh give me back my home!'

The parsonage is next to the churchyard, provoking Emily to '... see around me piteous tombstones grey, stretching their shadows far away'. Death stalked the Brontë family. The elder sisters, Maria and Elizabeth, died in 1825 and the younger children were weakened after an epidemic at their school. The writing careers

of the surviving sisters are remarkable for their brevity. Charlotte's *Jane Eyre*, Emily's *Wuthering Heights* and Anne's *Agnes Grey* were all published in 1847. Anne's *Tenant of Wildfell Hall* followed in 1848, shortly before the death of Emily (aged 30) and her brother Branwell. Anne died in 1849 aged 29, the year Charlotte's *Shirley* was published. Charlotte's *Villette* followed in 1852. Despite her father's strong opposition, Charlotte married the curate Arthur Bell Nicholls in 1854. She was dead within a year, however, at the age of 39, leaving only the Rev. Patrick Brontë, who died in 1861, aged 84.

C Haworth has retained its cobbled Main Street and the Black Bull Inn, where Branwell Brontë drank himself to death.

Walk 15
TOP WITHENS
5 miles (8 km) Moderate

The Brontës lived in what is now the museum in Haworth, but it is the neighbouring moors which really serve to represent their spirits and characters. This is a walk into their favourite wilderness, past places that are now inextricably linked with the Brontë name. Above all, this is the setting for Emily's great novel *Wuthering Heights*. The title aptly suggests an exposed, stormy place. Emily's novel is indeed about fierce passions in a confined world. Love and hatred are strong, as is jealousy, symbolised by the display of terrifying bitterness by the dying Cathy towards Heathcliff.

Of all the sisters, Emily had most affinity with her environment. She was known to be a passionate human being who kept to wild surroundings. Indeed, she became physically ill when elsewhere. As Charlotte wrote about her sister in the Preface to the 1850 edition of *Wuthering Heights*: 'her native hills were far more to her than a spectacle; they were what she lived in, and by, as much as the wild birds, their tenants, or as the heather, their produce.' Emily recorded her feelings towards the hills in *Wuthering Heights*: 'In winter, nothing more dreary, in summer nothing more divine, than those glens shut in by hills, and those bluff, bold swells of heather'.

Come in early March to experience the scene when the dying Cathy was brought crocuses by Edgar Linton: 'These are the earliest flowers at the Heights!' she exclaimed. 'They remind me of soft thaw winds, and warm sunshine, and nearly melted snow'. September is the time to see the mist, as Edgar and Cathy saw Wuthering Heights rise 'above this silver vapour'. Come in early November for 'a fresh watery afternoon, when the turf and paths were rustling with moist, withered leaves, and the cold, blue sky was half-hidden by clouds, dark grey streamers, rapidly mounting from the west and boding abundant rain'.

A hot July day is a reminder of Linton Heathcliff who enjoyed 'lying from morning to evening on a bank of heath in the middle of the moors, with the bees humming dreamily about among the bloom, and the larks singing high up overhead, and the blue sky and bright sun shining steadily and cloudlessly'.

The younger Cathy preferred 'rocking in a rustling green tree, with a west wind blowing, and bright, white clouds flitting rapidly above; and not only larks, but throstles, and blackbirds, and linnets, and cuckoos pouring out music on every side, and the moors seen at a distance, broken into cool dusky dells; but close by great swells of long grass undulating in waves to the breeze; and woods and sounding water, and the whole world awake and wild with joy.'

Come on this walk to step into the authentic atmosphere of Emily Brontë's *Wuthering Heights*. Roam where the motherless children found freedom from the stern discipline of their aunt and tuned into their imagination. This is the heart of Brontë country. This was what Emily Brontë probably had in mind when she wrote *The Sun has Set*:

'In all the lonely landscape round
I see no light and hear no sound
Except the wind that far away
Comes sighing o'er the heathy sea'.

This route can be linked with Walk 14.

A Brontë Bridge is an attractive clapper-type bridge across South Dean Beck. This simple slab bridge was washed away in the floods of May 1989, but re-erected soon afterwards.

B Although described by Charlotte Brontë, after one of her last walks, as 'a perfect torrent racing over the rocks', the Brontë Waterfalls are usually just a trickle of water.

C Top Withens is identified as the home of the Earnshaw family in Emily Brontë's *Wuthering Heights*.

D Ponden Hall is the Thrushcross Grange of *Wuthering Heights*.

Over

0   1 mile

0   1 km

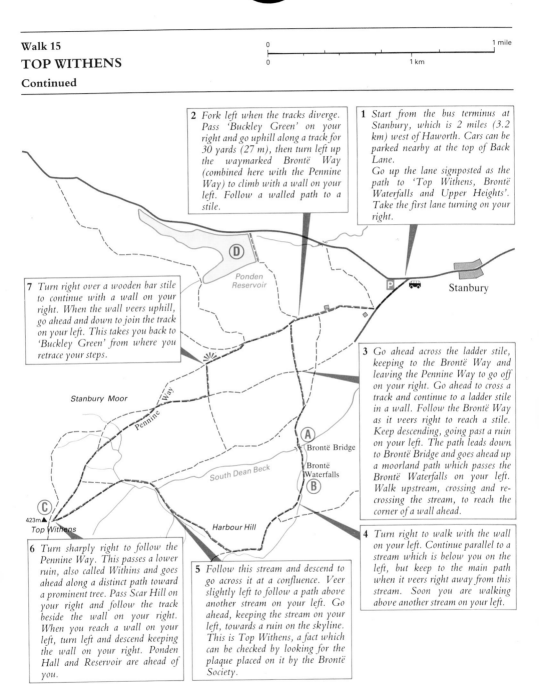

2 Fork left when the tracks diverge. Pass 'Buckley Green' on your right and go uphill along a track for 30 yards (27 m), then turn left up the waymarked Brontë Way (combined here with the Pennine Way) to climb with a wall on your left. Follow a walled path to a stile.

1 Start from the bus terminus at Stanbury, which is 2 miles (3.2 km) west of Haworth. Cars can be parked nearby at the top of Back Lane.
Go up the lane signposted as the path to 'Top Withens, Brontë Waterfalls and Upper Heights'. Take the first lane turning on your right.

Ponden Reservoir

Stanbury

7 Turn right over a wooden bar stile to continue with a wall on your right. When the wall veers uphill, go ahead and down to join the track on your left. This takes you back to 'Buckley Green' from where you retrace your steps.

3 Go ahead across the ladder stile, keeping to the Brontë Way and leaving the Pennine Way to go off on your right. Go ahead to cross a track and continue to a ladder stile in a wall. Follow the Brontë Way as it veers right to reach a stile. Keep descending, going past a ruin on your left. The path leads down to Brontë Bridge and goes ahead up a moorland path which passes the Brontë Waterfalls on your left. Walk upstream, crossing and re-crossing the stream, to reach the corner of a wall ahead.

Stanbury Moor

Pennine Way

Brontë Bridge

South Dean Beck

Brontë Waterfalls

423m▲
Top Withens

Harbour Hill

6 Turn sharply right to follow the Pennine Way. This passes a lower ruin, also called Withins and goes ahead along a distinct path toward a prominent tree. Pass Scar Hill on your right and follow the track beside the wall on your right. When you reach a wall on your left, turn left and descend keeping the wall on your right. Ponden Hall and Reservoir are ahead of you.

5 Follow this stream and descend to go across it at a confluence. Veer slightly left to follow a path above another stream on your left. Go ahead, keeping the stream on your left, towards a ruin on the skyline. This is Top Withens, a fact which can be checked by looking for the plaque placed on it by the Brontë Society.

4 Turn right to walk with the wall on your left. Continue parallel to a stream which is below you on the left, but keep to the main path when it veers right away from this stream. Soon you are walking above another stream on your left.

Walk 16

DRUID'S ALTAR

6 miles (9.7 km) Easy

During the Industrial Revolution the new towns of the South Pennines displayed great civic pride, with some mill owners genuinely concerned about the welfare of their employees. This altruism was based on strong religious beliefs. On this walk we pass a monument to one of those great reformers, and a place which was of great importance to the old religion of the druids.

A The Druid's Altar is part of spectacular crags formed by gritstone which outcrops above Airedale. Despite the urban nature of the valley, this is a superb view with Rombalds Moor as the backcloth. The course of the Leeds and Liverpool Canal can be traced on the far side of the River Aire. This is just the sort of place that druids would have used when making their sacrifices. It is fairly isolated, yet a bonfire here could be seen over a wide area. Such places were believed to have a certain power. Disraeli realised this and set a meeting of the Chartists here in his novel *Sybil*.

B The William Ferrand Monument was erected by his wife, Fanny Mary Ferrand, to commemorate his active support for the 10 hours Factory Bill restricting the length of the working day. As an MP he fought against the Truck System (payment by tokens exchangeable only at the company's shop, with its inflated prices) and advocated payment in current coins of the realm. A man of vision, he planted 400 acres (160 hectares) of trees and was MP for Knaresborough between 1841 and 1847 and for Devonport from 1863 to 1865. He died in 1889 in his 80th year.

C Lady Blantyre's Rock has a memorial stone on the spot where the Dowager Lady Blantyre came almost every summer for 30 years in the mid 19th century to read and enjoy the scenery. She died in her 84th year in 1875.

D The Local Authority now owns the country estate of St Ives. A turf research centre makes use of the facilities, where there is a nature trail through the magnificent woodland, a farm, a café and play area, a vast expanse of moor and a golf course.

Over

0   1 mile

0   1 km

3 *Look for a kissing-gate in the wall on your left, turn left through it and bear right diagonally to the corner of a projecting wall. Turn sharply left towards a pylon and go ahead through an old gateway and across the corner of the next field to a stile in a wall on your right.*

2 *Turn right along a track (Altar Lane) to follow a wall on your left to the top of the hill. When the trees break on your right at the top, bear right towards the crags of Druid's Altar. Notice the views across Airedale on your right as you follow the crag tops. Cross a track to go ahead over a stile and follow the panoramic path along Transfield Top.*

1 *Start from British Rail's station at Bingley, on the line between Leeds or Bradford and Skipton. If you come by car, Bingley is on the A650 between Bradford and Keighley, and you can park at the station. There are many bus services.*
From the station entrance, turn right along Wellington Street, then left up Park Road and turn right along Main Street. Turn left when you reach Mill Gate (opposite the fire station) and cross a bridge over the River Aire. Leave the road immediately by taking a steep path through the trees on your right.

Druid's Altar (A)

Lady Blantyre's Rock (B) (C)

Coppice Pond

St Ives (D)

River Aire

Harden Beck

Bingley

Station

4 *Turn left along Altar Lane, with a wall on your right. Reach a stile beside a gate on your right and go across it. Turn right again over another stile beside a gate to follow a track parallel to the wall on your right. Go ahead through a gate. Pass a pylon on your right to take the path through the trees near the wall on your right. Take a path on your left when you reach a wall ahead and go across a golf course, soon picking up a wall on your left. When the path forks, bear right to the William Ferrand Monument, with Lady Blantyre's Rock below it.*

5 *Turn right and descend along the path which bends left, parallel to the road, then bends left again to pass Coppice Pond on your left. Cross an estate road to follow a path ahead through a walled gateway. Fork right along the woodland path that zigzags down to a wall where you bear left, with the wall now on your right. Follow the track through the trees, with views over open fields on your right. Rejoin the estate road on your left at a lodge and bear right along it down towards the B6429.*

6 *Just after the estate road bends right, take a path through trees on your left, down to the B6429. Cross this road carefully and go ahead down Beckfoot Lane. Soon after passing houses on your right go ahead over a foot-bridge beside a ford and up the lane ahead. Pass allotments then turn left up a narrow path to a foot-bridge over the River Aire. Go ahead through Myrtle Park to emerge in Bingley's Main Street. Go left, then right at Chapel Lane back to the station.*

GOIT STOCK FALLS

6 miles (9.7 km) Moderate

This walk encompasses woodland (which, in May, is rich with bluebells), two waterfalls and an expanse of heather-clad moorland. The waterfalls will be at their best after a spell of wet weather. Harden Moor is owned by the local authority, so you can wander off the paths if you wish.

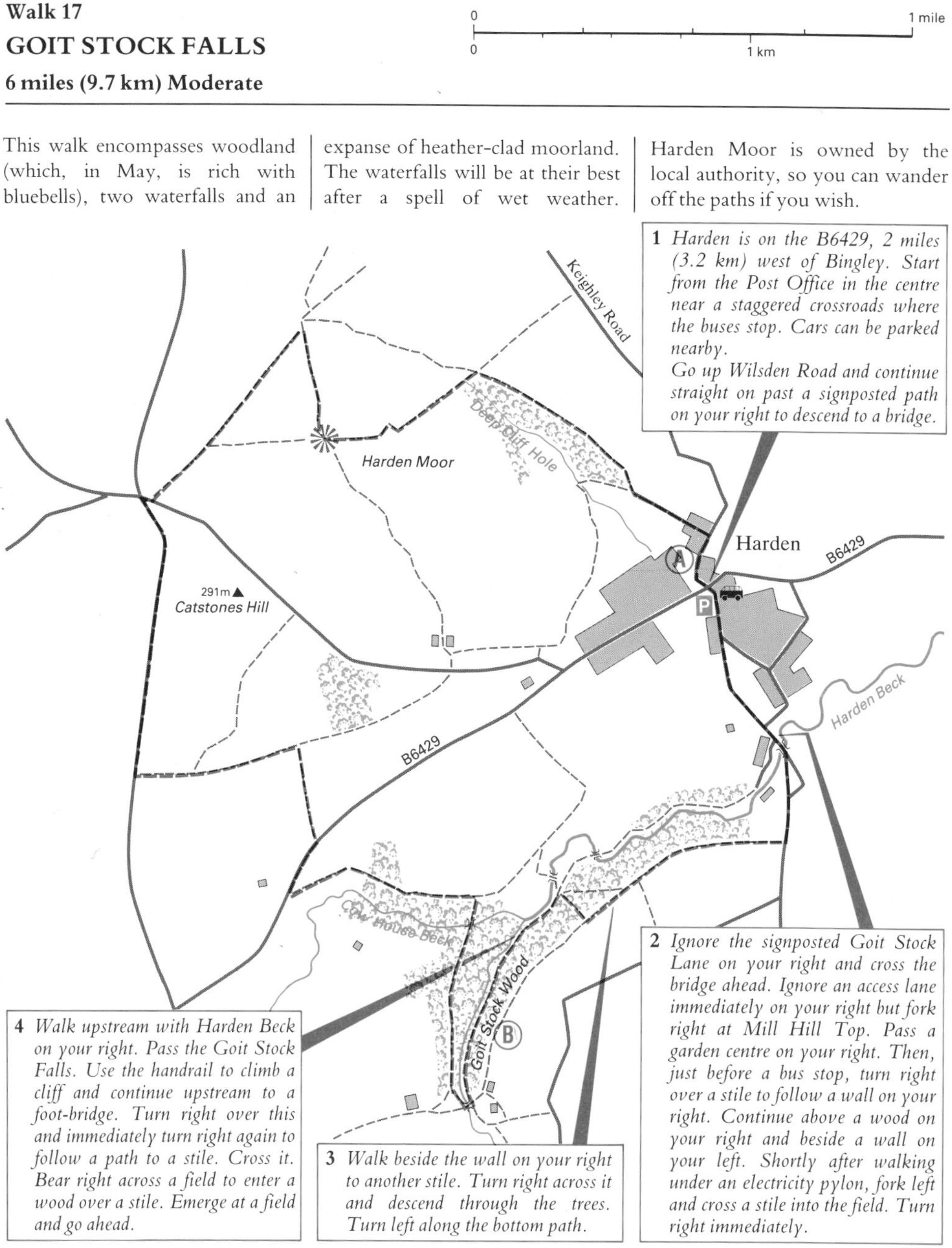

1 *Harden is on the B6429, 2 miles (3.2 km) west of Bingley. Start from the Post Office in the centre near a staggered crossroads where the buses stop. Cars can be parked nearby.*
Go up Wilsden Road and continue straight on past a signposted path on your right to descend to a bridge.

2 *Ignore the signposted Goit Stock Lane on your right and cross the bridge ahead. Ignore an access lane immediately on your right but fork right at Mill Hill Top. Pass a garden centre on your right. Then, just before a bus stop, turn right over a stile to follow a wall on your right. Continue above a wood on your right and beside a wall on your left. Shortly after walking under an electricity pylon, fork left and cross a stile into the field. Turn right immediately.*

3 *Walk beside the wall on your right to another stile. Turn right across it and descend through the trees. Turn left along the bottom path.*

4 *Walk upstream with Harden Beck on your right. Pass the Goit Stock Falls. Use the handrail to climb a cliff and continue upstream to a foot-bridge. Turn right over this and immediately turn right again to follow a path to a stile. Cross it. Bear right across a field to enter a wood over a stile. Emerge at a field and go ahead.*

Over

34

0   1 mile

0   1 km

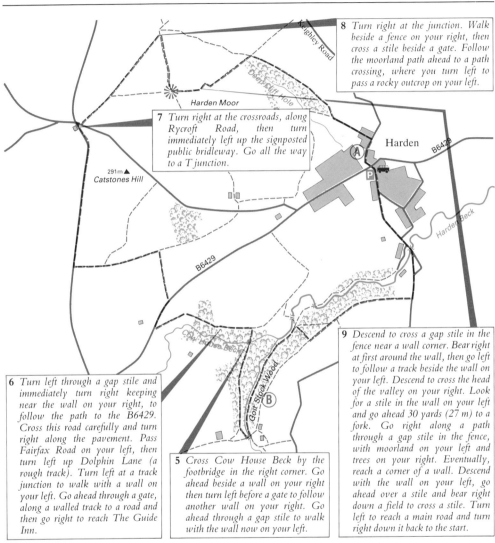

8 Turn right at the junction. Walk beside a fence on your right, then cross a stile beside a gate. Follow the moorland path ahead to a path crossing, where you turn left to pass a rocky outcrop on your left.

7 Turn right at the crossroads, along Rycroft Road, then turn immediately left up the signposted public bridleway. Go all the way to a T junction.

Harden Moor

Harden

291m ▲
Catstones Hill

B6429

B6429

Harden Beck

Cow House Beck

Goit Stock Wood

9 Descend to cross a gap stile in the fence near a wall corner. Bear right at first around the wall, then go left to follow a track beside the wall on your left. Descend to cross the head of the valley on your right. Look for a stile in the wall on your left and go ahead 30 yards (27 m) to a fork. Go right along a path through a gap stile in the fence, with moorland on your left and trees on your right. Eventually, reach a corner of a wall. Descend with the wall on your left, go ahead over a stile and bear right down a field to cross a stile. Turn left to reach a main road and turn right down it back to the start.

6 Turn left through a gap stile and immediately turn right keeping near the wall on your right, to follow the path to the B6429. Cross this road carefully and turn right along the pavement. Pass Fairfax Road on your left, then turn left up Dolphin Lane (a rough track). Turn left at a track junction to walk with a wall on your left. Go ahead through a gate, along a walled track to a road and then go right to reach The Guide Inn.

5 Cross Cow House Beck by the footbridge in the right corner. Go ahead beside a wall on your right then turn left before a gate to follow another wall on your right. Go ahead through a gap stile to walk with the wall now on your left.

A Harden is a large village close to Bingley, with a factory which makes parts for cars. The workers must enjoy the close proximity of such exhilarating countryside. It is easy to understand how the rambling movement began in the industrial north.

B Here, in beautiful Goit Stock Wood, are the Goit Stock Falls.

Walk 18

OXENHOPE

5.5 miles (8.9 km) Moderate/strenuous

Leeming Reservoir, Thornton Moor Reservoir, Warley Moor Reservoir and Leeshaw Reservoir are all prominent landmarks on this walk, supplying water to the large towns of West Yorkshire, and changing a landscape which was once familiar to the Brontës. Keep a look out for moorland birds.

A The church of St Mary the Virgin at Oxenhope was built in 1849, thanks to the remarkable efforts of the Rev. Joseph Brett Grant. As a recently appointed curate, he was asked by the Rev. Patrick Brontë of Haworth in 1845 to take charge of a newly formed parish here. Services were at first held in a wool combing shop and money was raised to build a school. The curate was to wear out 14 pairs of shoes over the next few years as he zealously collected the money for this church. Charlotte Brontë took him as her model for the Rev. Donne, who was 'unsurpassed in the art of begging'. The church's foundation stone was laid on St Valentine's Day, 1849, and the building was consecrated on 11th October of the same year. The Rev. Grant stayed here for the rest of his life, dying in November 1879, at the age of 59. He was so popular that the 437 seats in his church could not accommodate all the parishioners who wished to attend his funeral service.

B Oxenhope is a neat little Pennine mill town, seemingly unaffected by the tourist appeal of its neighbour, Haworth, and with much to see, including traditional weavers' cottages (recognisable by their mullioned windows). The prime attraction is the railway station. Here you can visit the railway museum with its impressive collection of steam locomotives, rolling stock and memorabilia. It would be appropriate to make the steam powered Keighley and Worth Valley Railway your means of access to the start of this walk (it links with British Rail at Keighley). Check train times by telephoning 0535 43629. Services operate every weekend throughout the year, and on weekdays during the summer. You have probably already seen this famous little railway – on the screen. It was a location for *The Railway Children, Yanks, A Woman of Substance* and *The Adventures of Sherlock Holmes*.

The line climbs continuously at an average gradient of 1 in 75 for 5 miles from Keighley to its terminus at Oxenhope. It wasn't easy to build, with two years' hard labour needed to overcome the steep slopes, the streams and the dense, boggy woodland. The Brontë sisters were all dead by the time the first train ran on this line in 1867, although they lived in the 1840s when railway mania took a grip on the land.

When Charlotte and Anne Brontë travelled to London to visit the publishers Smith, Elder and Company, in 1848 (in order to prove their separate identity after another publisher, Newby, had implied that Anne's novel *The Tenant of Wildfowl Hall* [published by Newby] was by the same author as *Jane Eyre* [written by Charlotte and published by Smith, Elder & Company]), they were able to go by train from Keighley. There was a plan at that time for a railway to link Keighley and Colne via Trawden and Haworth. The plan was dropped, however, leaving the mill owners in the Worth Valley to conduct long negotiations for a purely local line. The railway was to cater for the tourists who had read the works of the Brontës and wanted to visit where they had lived and set their novels. British Rail closed the line in 1961. The Keighley and Worth Valley Railway Preservation Society was formed, and they reopened the line in 1968, making the railway once again part of Valley life.

Over

0   1 mile

0   1 km

1 *Start from the Keighley & Worth Valley Railway's station at Oxenhope. Take the steam train to here from Keighley, which is served by many buses. Oxenhope is situated at the junction of the* A6033 *and the* B6141, *5 miles (8 km) south of Keighley.*

Go straight ahead from the station, crossing Mill Lane carefully. Walk up Station Road to reach the Post Office, on your left. Go ahead along the B6141 towards Denholme, then veer right up Jew Lane. Do not take the first fork on your right (down to a factory), but take the second, down a 'No Through Road'.

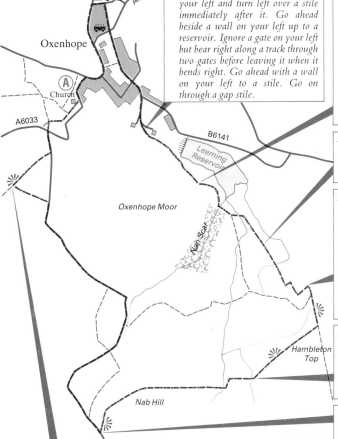

Station 🅟 🅑 A6033

Oxenhope

🅐
Church

A6033

B6141

Leeming Reservoir

Oxenhope Moor

Nan Scar

Hambleton Top

Nab Hill

2 *Follow the track past a house on your left and turn left over a stile immediately after it. Go ahead beside a wall on your left up to a reservoir. Ignore a gate on your left but bear right along a track through two gates before leaving it when it bends right. Go ahead with a wall on your left to a stile. Go on through a gap stile.*

3 *Walk with a fence on your left and a wall on your right to a gap stile ahead. Continue until you meet a wall on your left. Go through a door and descend with this wall. Turn left over a footbridge and continue uphill to a wall corner then down to cross a bridge on your left. Turn right to walk upstream (with the stream on your right). Go ahead through a gap stile and continue with a wall on your left.*

4 *Continue walking uphill over two stiles and across a footbridge. Go up a walled path which bends left, then right, then left again.*

5 *Turn right along a track. Continue over a stile beside a gate along a walled track. Look for a break in the wall on your right, opposite an old gateway in the wall on your left (over which you can see Thornton Moor Reservoir). Turn right here along a moorland path. There are fine views of Leeming Reservoir and Oxenhope on your right.*

6 *Go ahead over a stream and walk with the remains of a wall on your right. Go around the head of the next clough, pass old quarry ruins and bear left to see Warley Moor Reservoir. Walk down to the lane.*

7 *Turn right to follow the lane to a radio mast. Pass a pond on your left, then a gate, then turn left over steps in the wall. Walk with a wall on your left and Leeshaw Reservoir ahead of you.*

8 *Cross a stile and turn right down a track to the lane. Bear left to the* A6033. *Cross carefully to the track opposite. Turn right to the* church. Go down to the road and bear left back to Oxenhope. Turn right at Mill Lane to return to the station on your left.

Walk 19
SALTAIRE
2.5 miles (4 km) Easy

0   1 mile

0   1 km

Saltaire derived its name from Sir Titus Salt, the mill-owner and from the River Aire. It is an excellent example of benevolent capitalism. Built in the wake of the Chartist uprising, it was designed both to improve the living conditions of the workers and to make them acquiescent. This gentle stroll beside river and canal must have been a favourite means of relaxation for Saltaire's workers.

3 *Pass a foot-bridge over the river on your left and go ahead under a tunnel formed by a pipe bridge. Cross a foot-bridge over a tributary ahead and pass between the river and boat houses.*

2 *Cross the canal bridge and go ahead across the footbridge over the River Aire. Turn left to walk upstream with the river on your left. Pass the cricket ground on your right, then leave the park and* walk through fields keeping close to the river.

1 *Saltaire is on the A650 just north of Bradford. Considerate street parking is possible. Start from British Rail's station at Saltaire, on the Skipton to Leeds or Bradford line. There are also bus services.*
Go left from the station to pass Titus Salt's mill on your right.

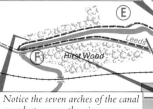

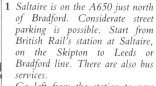

4 *Notice the seven arches of the canal aqueduct across the river on your left. Climb up to the canal bank and turn left across the aqueduct.*

5 *Walk along the towpath with the Leeds and Liverpool Canal on your right all the way back to Saltaire.*

6 *Turn right over the bridge across the canal and walk up the road past Titus Salt's mill on your left. The British Rail station is down on your right.*

A This is the mill built by Sir Titus Salt and which dominated his village. Completed in 1853, its construction enabled production to be increased and the workforce to be rehoused away from the slums, vice and pollution of inner Bradford. At its peak the mill held 1200 looms capable of weaving 30,000 yards (9100 m) of cloth every day. It employed over 3000 people.

B The Congregational (now United Reformed) church, built by Sir Titus Salt, was opened in 1859. It is a superb building with Corinthian style columns, a tower, a dome and a startling interior.

C Sir James Roberts, who was the subsequent owner of the firm founded by Sir Titus Salt, presented Roberts Park to the City of Bradford in 1920. The park was originally set out as part of Saltaire by Sir Titus Salt, whose statue (erected in 1903, 27 years after Salt's death) stands by its main terrace. The statue also commemorates the llama and alpaca, whose fleeces made Salt's fortune. The park is a good example of Salt's paternalism. The provision of organised leisure activities was generous, but the accent was on control. Games could not be played on Sundays, and gambling and swearing were not allowed at any time.

D Cricket is taken very seriously in Yorkshire. This ground is where Jim Laker started his spin bowling career in 1938.

E This stretch of river is where Bradford Grammar School Rowing Club is based.

F The Seven Arches carry the Leeds and Liverpool Canal over the River Aire at this point.

G This is the famous model village built by Sir Titus Salt to house his mill workers. It took from 1851 to 1872 to construct and had its own almshouses, church and hospital. There was no public house, however. Its station opened in 1859, closed in 1965 and reopened in 1983.

Walk 20

DENHOLME

5.5 miles (8.9 km) Moderate

0 — 1 mile
0 — 1 km

This is a varied and interesting walk. There are particularly good views over Brontë country at the end of Thornton Moor Road (which is an unsurfaced track).

6 *Reach the B6141 and go left. Turn right over a stile. Go ahead to cross a stile and bear right beside a wall on your right. Maintain this direction through two stiles and with a wall now on your left. Ignore a farm track on your right and turn left to walk with a wall on your left to a stile. Cross it and turn right to walk beside a wall on your right. Go ahead to descend to Denholme by way of Edge Bottom.*

1 *Start from the bus stop near the Old Black Bull, Denholme, on the A629, 7 miles (11.3 km) north of Halifax. Motorists may prefer to start from the car park near Doe Park Reservoir (at no. 2). Walk towards Halifax and turn left down Foster Park (signposted to the sailing centre). Follow* Foster Park View *and go down to the reservoir on your left.*

2 *Pass a car park on your right and cross the dam ahead. Turn right along a track. Veer left through a kissing-gate to continue along the path above the reservoir on your right. Cross a stile in the bottom corner and turn right to take a walled path around the head of the reservoir to a foot-bridge. Cross this and turn left.*

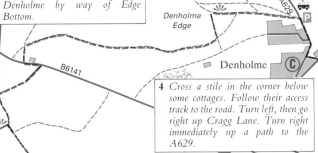

Denholme Edge

B6141

Denholme

Denholme Edge

P

A629

P

Doe Park

(A)

Doe Park Reservoir

4 *Cross a stile in the corner below some cottages. Follow their access track to the road. Turn left, then go right up Cragg Lane. Turn right immediately up a path to the A629.*

Stubden Reservoir

(B)

Denholme Beck

Thornton Moor Reservoir

Thornton Moor Road

Thornton Moor

A629

Denholme Gate

3 *Walk upstream near a beck on your left. Continue under the dismantled Keighley to Halifax railway. Continue straight ahead with the beck on your left. Cross the beck at some stepping stones.*

5 *Cross the road carefully and go ahead up Black Edge Lane, which becomes Thornton Moor Road.* Walk past the reservoir and reach a T junction. Turn right along a tarmac track which bears left.

A Doe Park Reservoir is usually busy with brightly coloured yachts each weekend. This is a popular sailing centre.

B The dismantled railway line which crosses your route here was the route between Keighley and Halifax, via Queensbury.

C Although Denholme has had its central mill demolished, it still retains the atmosphere of a mill village.

THORNTON

4 miles (6.4 km) Moderate

0   1 mile

0   1 km

Only marvellous views of the city in the east betray the fact that this walk is on the fringe of Bradford. You descend and ascend a rural dale with the beck, or stream, which becomes the notorious beck under Bradford (t'mucky beck) still pristine and spanned here by a stone slab bridge. The views from the Allerton Road are excellent.

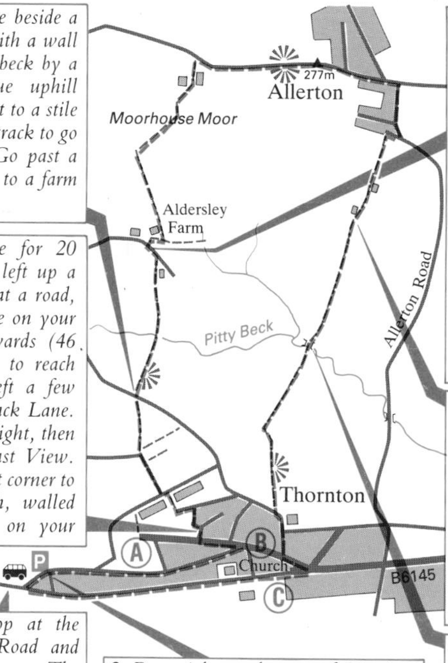

4 *Cross a lane, and a stile beside a gate ahead, to descend with a wall on your left. Cross the beck by a foot-bridge and continue uphill with a wall on your right to a stile in the top field. Cross a track to go ahead through a gate. Go past a farmhouse on your right to a farm roadway.*

3 *Walk up May Avenue for 20 yards (18 m) and turn left up a narrow path. Turn left at a road, passing Northcliffe Close on your right. Then, after 50 yards (46 m), turn right up steps to reach Sapgate Lane. Turn left a few paces and go right up Back Lane. Pass Hill Croft on your right, then pass a track down to East View. Leave the lane at the next corner to go ahead down a rough, walled track, ignoring a track on your right.*

1 *Start from the bus stop at the junction of Thornton Road and Lower Kipping Lane, near The Wellington, at Thornton. Motorists will find Thornton on the B6145, 4 miles (6.4 km) west of Bradford. Street parking is possible.*
With your back to The Wellington, turn right to the junction, then go left uphill along Kipping Lane.

2 *Bear right at the top of Kipping Lane, to go along High Street. Look on the left for no 74, which is marked by a plaque recording that four of the Brontës were born here. Continue along Brontë Old Road. Turn left up Spring Head Road and pass Northcliffe Avenue before turning right up May Avenue.*

local curate from 1815 to 1820.

5 *Go left to a junction. Turn right to pass houses on your left and turn left up a narrow path. Continue beside a wall on your right. Turn right over a stile in the top corner and walk with a wall on your left. Cross a beck and climb to a corner where you turn left over a stile. Go ahead to a stile in a corner on your right. Cross it and take a walled path to a track. Bear left to a road, where you turn right along Allerton Road. Turn right up Cote Lane. Ignore Egerton Grove but turn right on a track to Bailey Fold.*

6 *Pass the farmhouse on your right. Veer right to a gate and go through the right-hand one of two lower gates. Descend with a wall on your left until you are half way down the third field, where you cross a stile to continue with the wall on your right. Cross a foot-bridge over the beck below and veer left to cross a stile ahead.*

7 *Climb with a wall on your left to the top of the second field. Turn left over a stile to reach another stile leading to a walled track on your right. Follow this through a farmyard to a road. Continue past The Northcliffe and down Northcliffe Lane. Turn left down Spring Head Road to Thornton Road, where you go right to the church, and return to The Wellington.*

A Four of the Brontës were born at no 74 High Street: Charlotte on 21st April, 1816; Patrick Branwell on 26th June, 1817; Emily Jane on 30th July, 1818; Anne on 17th January, 1820. Their father was the

B The church of St James was consecrated in 1872.

C The ruins of the old church, known as the Bell Chapel, are across the road. This is where the Rev. Patrick Brontë was curate and where the children were christened. This church dates back to at least 1612.

Map labels: Moorhouse Moor, 277m, Allerton, Aldersley Farm, Pitty Beck, Allerton Road, Thornton, Church, B6145, B6145, A, B, C, P

MARSDEN

3 miles (4.8 km) Easy

The mill town of Marsden is set in magnificent scenery, with reservoirs in the south pointing towards the nearby Peak District.

This area is a prime example of the wilderness which characterises the Pennines. The scenery is dramatic, and so is the history of the people.

Luddites took their secret oaths here and vowed to fight the mill owners.

Marsden

1 *Start from British Rail's station at Marsden. This is on the line between Manchester and Leeds via Huddersfield. Buses stop here, while motorists will find space to park nearby. Marsden is on the A62, 7 miles (11.3 km) west of Huddersfield.*
Cross the bridge over the canal and go down Station Road.

2 *Fork right, across a bridge over the River Colne and pass the church on your right. Pass Towngate on your left and, ignoring a road on your right, go ahead across a bridge over a stream, and then under the bridge which carries the A62 road. Reach a roundabout and go up Binn Road.*

3 *Bear right up the signposted path past the mill. Reach a public footpath signpost at the end of the path and turn left up steps. At the top turn right along a road and fork right onto the path to the reservoir.*

8 *Turn left down a walled path. This bears right above a farmhouse. Go down steps on your left and through a small gate ahead. Turn left through the farmyard and follow a track on your right to the town. Walk down Peel Street, turn left over a bridge and up Station Road.*

4 *Walk with the reservoir on your right until you are nearly level with the start of the conifer trees on the other side of the reservoir.*

7 *Turn sharply left up the track to Acrehead Farm. Just before the track starts to bend right, turn left over a stile near the National Trust sign for Binn Moor. Go down the signposted footpath. Descend to cross a stile in the wall below and keep descending to reach a stile in the fence on your left. Cross it to go down a walled path.*

5 *Turn left through a gap stile and walk up a walled path away from the reservoir. Continue with a wall on your right and a view through oak trees over the reservoir on your left. Bear right with the wall to a path junction.*

6 *Go left along the walled path. Pass a farmhouse on your left and continue down to a lane. Turn right to follow the lane around a hairpin bend.*

A This is the Huddersfield Narrow Canal. Built between 1795 and 1811, it linked Manchester with Huddersfield. Although not quite 20 miles (32 km) long, it had 74 locks, five aqueducts and two tunnels, including Standedge, the longest canal tunnel in Britain.

B When you pass the churchyard on your right, notice a grassy area in front of modern flats to your left. The ruins of a former church can be seen, and just to the right of these is the monument to Enoch and James Taylor. These brothers were blacksmiths who made the shearing frames which were making the highly skilled croppers redundant, and turning them into Luddites. The Luddites never attacked those who made the machines, such as the Taylors, but turned their attentions to the mill owners.

HOLMBRIDGE

5 miles (8.0 km) Moderate

0   1 mile
0   1 km

The Holme Valley is a beautiful area for walking. Field paths and tracks, woodland and the attractive Holme Styes Reservoir combine to make this an invigorating, varied walk. There are fine views down the Holme Valley and across the cloughs and moors. A remote cricket ground stands as a witness to the passion for the game in Yorkshire. Look out for kestrels.

1 *Start from the bus stop near the Post Office in Holmbridge. This is where the no. 310 bus service from Huddersfield stops. Motorists will find Holmbridge on the A6024, 8 miles (12.9 km) south of Huddersfield. Cars can be parked near the Post Office, which is facing the church and has the cricket ground on its right.*
Walk past the church on your left to cross the bridge over the River Holme.

3 *Bear right along a woodland path to steps on your left. Go down these and walk ahead to cross the stream (Dobb Dike) by a footbridge. Climb up to cross a stile in the corner and cross a road to Acre Lane opposite. Walk along this lane, with fine views over the Holme Valley on your left. Turn right up Hill House Lane (a rough, grassy track).*

4 *Bear left with Hill House Lane in front of the houses to reach a road junction. Take the uphill road ahead. This bends right to a crossroads, where you turn right past the cricket ground on your right. Notice the tall, slim, windmill on your left. Pass the football pitch on your left and turn left over a stile to walk with a wall on your left towards the windmill. Cross a stile in the corner to reach a lane.*

2 *Fork left, then turn right up the road signposted to Yateholme. Passing the Fernleigh Restaurant, go ahead up Brownhill Lane for a few paces, then turn left up a signposted path. Turn left at the houses and follow the lane to pass through a gate leading to another gate. Go through this gate, ignoring a stile 10 yards (9 m) to its right. Go ahead beside a wall on your left to climb a stile beside a gate. Cross the foot of a second field to cross a stile in the corner. Continue past houses on your left to climb another stile.*

5 *Turn right along this lane until it meets another path at a T junction. Turn sharp left and follow the path as it turns right to meet another T junction. Turn left and continue to a third T Junction. Turn right here and proceed until a path to the left leads into Fox Clough. Follow this past a path which joins from the left. A sharp right turn is followed by a sharp left turn through a wicket gate.*

River Holme

P

Holmbridge

Church

Cricket Ground

Dobb Dike

Cartworth Moor Road

Cartworth Moor

Fox Clough

Holmstyes Reservoir

B

A

Over

0 _____ 1 mile

0 _____ 1 km

11 Go ahead with a wall on your left, pass trees on your right and maintain this direction, passing through a gate, until you reach a farm track on your right. Ignore it, going ahead through a small gate to the walled path which leads to a stile on your right. Cross this and veer right to descend to a wooded gully. Follow the path to the houses passed near the start. Retrace your steps to Holmbridge.

6 Walk close to the beck on your right, ignoring the first bridge over it. Just before a second bridge, veer left as directed by a public footpath signpost and descend to a third foot-bridge. Turn right over this and climb with a wall on your left and up steps to another public footpath signpost. Continue up a rough lane to a road, where you bear right for 250 yards (229 m) to a corner. Bear right down a rough walled track above the reservoir on your right.

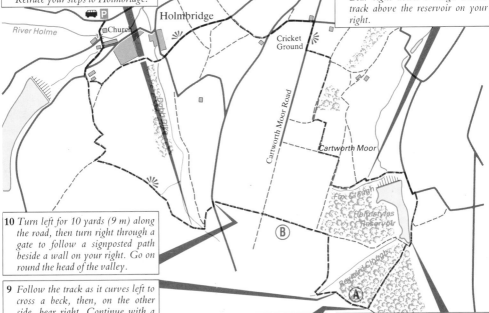

10 Turn left for 10 yards (9 m) along the road, then turn right through a gate to follow a signposted path beside a wall on your right. Go on round the head of the valley.

9 Follow the track as it curves left to cross a beck, then, on the other side, bear right. Continue with a wall on your left and trees on your right. Turn left at a T junction, cross a stile to follow a walled track away from the forest. Go ahead at a crosstracks and eventually reach a road.

8 Go ahead through a gate (or use the stile to its right) and turn right along a track. Pass two lots of ruined buildings on your right and veer slightly left to walk with a wall on your right.

7 Fork right down to the head of the reservoir. Cross a stile beside a gate and go left uphill through the conifer trees. Keep to the main forest track, ignoring a forest ride on your left.

A You will come across some strange place-names in the South Pennines. This is Hades, described by Virgil as 'a gloomy, sunless abode where the ghosts of the dead flit about like bats'. No wonder it's a ruin!

B This is Elysium, where 'the souls of the virtuous enjoy complete happiness and innocent pleasures.'

RYBURN RESERVOIR

5.8 miles (9.3 km) Easy

0   1 mile

0   1 km

Reservoirs are the theme of this walk, on which you will cross two spectacular dams. Your outward journey is fairly level, beside or parallel to the River Ryburn, which is a tributary of the Calder. The path around an arm of Ryburn Reservoir is delightfully wooded. It is followed by field paths with fine views. The return is made along quiet lanes which overlook the valley.

6 *Cross the dam and the A58. Go uphill alongside the car park to a lane and turn right. Pass the Blue Bell Inn on your left and go left at a fork. Bear right at the next fork, then turn right up a lane which then bends left. Go ahead at a crossroads. Continue across a second crossroads to descend to Ripponden. Bear left along Spring Street and down Back Lane to reach The Golden Lion.*

1 *Ripponden is easily reached by bus (560, 568 from Halifax or Rochdale and 556 from Halifax or Manchester). Motorists will find it at the junction of the A58 and the A672, 5 miles (8 km) south of Halifax, and can park near the church.*
Start from the bus stop near the Golden Lion. Walk down Elland Road, overlooking the packhorse bridge on your left.

2 *Turn left towards St Bartholomew's church and turn sharp left again through Millfold Yard, passing the packhorse bridge on your right. Go ahead under the road bridge you have just crossed to follow a path beside the River Ryburn on your right.*

5 *Reach a narrow inlet and turn right over a foot-bridge to continue up a woodland path with steps to a field. Walk with a wall on your right, following the waymarks. Pass a farm on your left and continue to a signpost at the corner. Turn right to a ruin and then go left into a waymarked track. Fork right through a waymarked gate to a farm. Turn right down a track to the dam of Baitings Reservoir.*

4 *Go ahead along Bar Lane for 1000 yards (914 m) to reach a mill and take the signposted path under the archway and uphill. At the next bend in the lane take the path to the left of the large garage building and go forward to a stile and flight of steps. Go up these steps to the reservoir. Cross the dam. Take a woodland path on the right.*

3 *Soon after you pass a foot-bridge on the right, turn left up steps and then turn right to walk with a fence on your left. Continue forward above the river on your right. Turn left with this path to a lane and go right to cross the bridge and pass a mill on your left. Turn right along the A672 very briefly to the bridge over the River Ryburn. Turn left and cross the A672 to Bar Lane.*

A Ripponden is an ancient river crossing. The Romans probably used a ford where the old packhorse bridge now stands. This bridge dates back to the aftermath of a great flood in 1722. The original stone packhorse bridge was built in 1533.

B A Roman road ran along this lane.

Walk 25

RIPPONDEN

3.3 miles (5.3 km) Easy

0 _____ 1 mile

0 _____ 1 km

The Calderdale Way is a fine example of a medium distance waymarked route. It runs for 50 miles (80 km) around Calderdale, including the valley of its tributary, the Ryburn, with a fine network of link paths. This short walk follows the route from Ripponden to Mill Bank. The return is made beside a stream and near the river, on level paths shaded by trees.

3 *Turn left through a gap stile and bear left along a walled path, known as Cow Lane. This leads to Soyland Town. Turn right along a road for 300 yards (274 m), then turn right through a waymarked gate and follow a paved path to a stile. Turn right down a track which bends left. Turn left at a signpost to go over a stile and downhill. Walk with a wall on your right, then down steps near the bottom. Bear left to a lane and turn right to Mill Bank.*

2 *Turn right along a waymarked path. This is part of the Calderdale Way, which is waymarked with a 'c' above a 'w'. Bear left over a waymarked stile beside a gate and bear right with a wall on your right to go through a gate ahead. Continue along a paved path. Ignore paths to right and left to continue over a stile with a wall on the left and a fine view on the right.*

1 *Start from St Bartholomew's church, Ripponden. This is near the junction of the A58 and the A672, 5 miles (8 km) south of Halifax. Cars can be parked nearby, and buses run to Ripponden from Manchester (no 556) and Halifax (nos 556, 560 and 568).*
Turn right over the packhorse bridge and walk up to the A58. Go ahead up Royd Lane for 300 yards (274 m).

4 *The Calderdale Way goes left from Mill Bank. Leave its waymarks here by turning right just before the bridge. Walk with the stream on your left, bearing right along the upper path through woodland.*

5 *Go ahead through a gap stile at the end of the wood and pass a mill on your left. Bear right down a track to the A58 and turn right along the pavement. Soon after a bus shelter on your left, turn left.*

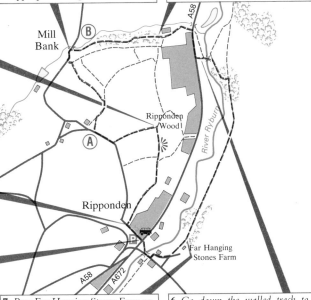

Mill Bank

Ripponden Wood

Ripponden

Far Hanging Stones Farm

A58   A672

7 *Pass Far Hanging Stones Farm on your left. Continue to a road and bear right downhill back to St Bartholomew's church.*

6 *Go down the walled track to a fork, where you bear right and cross a foot-bridge over the river. Bear right along a woodland path. Go left over a bridge across a dismantled railway and bear right downhill.*

A Making Place, Soyland, was once a thriving centre of the cottage weaving industry. Later, commercial skills were taught here.

B Mill Bank is now a conservation area. What was used to power its manorial corn mill and the 14th-century fulling mills.

DENBY DALE

3.8 miles (6.1 km) Moderate

0				1 mile
0		1 km		

The 'Pie Country' (see below) of Denby Dale is in an area often neglected by tourists, even though the countryside is delightful and the footpaths are well maintained and easily reached by public transport. Woodland, parkland and old tracks all feature on this walk, in an out of the way corner of Yorkshire notable for its little narrow paths, or ginnels.

8 Walk with a wall on your right to a lane. Cross a stile facing you and veer left to a fenced path. Go ahead to a corner and turn left. Turn left again at a house to pass through a gate on your right. Go along a track across the railway and back to the station.

1 Start from British Rail's station at Denby Dale, which is on the scenic Penistone line between Huddersfield and Sheffield. Many buses stop nearby, and you can park here. Denby Dale is near the junction of the A635 and the A636, 8 miles (12.9 km) southeast of Huddersfield.
Turn right as you leave the station but soon fork left down a rough track.

2 Emerge at The Prospect pub on the A636. Turn left, then cross the road on your right to go down Norman Road. Go ahead across the road at the bottom and go up Trinity Drive. Pass the church on your right and follow the surfaced path ahead to cross a field to a road. Turn left for 20 yards (18 m), then turn right up Broombank. Bear right along the ginnel near the end of this street.

3 Go under the railway and through a gate to walk straight across a field to a wood. Go over a stile and turn left along a walled track. Go ahead to a crosstracks.

4 Turn right along another walled track. Bear left around the edge of a wood, ignoring gates on your right. The path veers right after the trees, going beside a wall on your left. Go ahead over a stile to continue with a wall on your right.

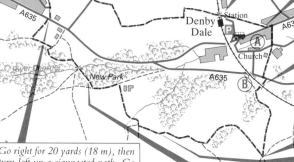

7 Go right for 20 yards (18 m), then turn left up a signposted path. Go right at a street, then left to continue along a path in your previous direction. Ignore a path on your right and pass a church to reach a road. Turn right to follow this road almost to the edge of the village. Turn right along a path that is signposted between two red-brick bungalows. Go ahead with a hedge on your left for 50 yards (46 m) then veer left to reach a stile in the wall corner.

6 Cut across the corner of a field to cross the foot-bridge over the River Dearne. Go into the field where crossing a stile on your left leads to a path across a beck and through trees to re-cross the beck on your right. Take a track on your right for 50 yards (46 m), then turn left along a path above the trees. Turn right up a ginnel to reach the A635.

5 Follow the walled track in the corner. Just before it ends at a gate, turn right over a stile and follow a wall on your right. Cross a beck and walk with a wall on your right to a stile. Bear right along a track. Pass a farm on your right. When the track turns right, go left through a gate. Walk under the trees near a wall on your left. When this wall comes closer, bear right down to cross a stile in the wall ahead.

A Denby Dale is famous for its giant meat pies. The first one was made in 1788 to celebrate the recovery of King George III from mental illness. The September 1988 pie is reputed to have provided 40,000 portions. An old pie dish is now a flower container.

B This viaduct carries British Rail's Penistone Line. The stations along this scenic route are great favourites with ramblers.

SCAPEGOAT HILL

3 miles (4.8 km) Easy

0   1 mile

0   1 km

Scapegoat Hill's name is actually derived from 'sheep-cote'. It is one of the highest villages in Yorkshire, at an altitude of 1100 feet (330 m) above sea level. The views from this walk are extensive and include the M62, which provides surprisingly fascinating company from the distance of Hall Lane. The Romans came this way too, building a fort at Slack.

5 *Take a path ahead and bear right beside a wall on your left to the clubhouse. Retrace your steps to the bridge and cross it. Bear left up a waymarked path. Go through a gap stile and turn right to walk uphill to climb a stile in a corner.*

4 *When the track bears left to re-cross the brook, go straight ahead along a narrow woodland path above the brook on your left. Keep to the upper path, above the trees, ignoring another fork leading down to the brook. Reach a bridge wide enough for golf course vehicles.*

3 *Follow the walled path through the wood to its edge and take the right fork. Continue across a corner of the golf course, taking a waymarked path through a gate. Go across the golf course to a post where the path enters woodland and take a path which joins from your right. Bear left over a bridge across Longwood Brook. Go straight ahead at a path junction, ignoring a right turn.*

2 *Continue with a wall on your right to go through a small gate and cut across the corner of a field. Go through another gate which leads to a lane. Turn right and, almost immediately, fork left downhill towards the reservoirs. Follow the paved lane as it bends right, then sharply left to pass above houses on your right. Go ahead to a wood.*

1 *Scapegoat Hill is 3 miles (4.8 km) west of Huddersfield. Start from the terminus of the no. 303 bus from Huddersfield, near a shop at the corner of High Street and Chapel Street. Parking space is nearby.*
Start by walking up New Lane. After the first field beyond houses on your right, turn right through a gap stile in the corner of the next field. Walk diagonally across the field to a small gate in the far corner.

6 *Turn left to a farm and turn right up Hall Lane, a walled track with views over the M62 on your right. Reach a road and turn sharply left. Look for a stone at a road junction.*

7 *At the road junction, go ahead along School Lane. Turn left down Chapel Street back to the start of the walk.*

A Upper Longwood Reservoir was built in 1848 to supply water to the rapidly increasing population of Huddersfield.

B This reservoir, on the Longwood Brook, was built in 1827 and enlarged in 1845. Its purpose was to maintain a supply of water to the woollen mills downstream.

C Stone tenter posts, used when the woollen industry was based in local cottages, can be found in Pighill Wood.

D The golf clubhouse stands on the site of a Roman fort built by Agricola in AD78.

E This stone was erected in 1756.

BRETTON HALL

3.5 miles (5.6 km) Easy

0   1 mile

0   1 km

The parkland of an 18th-century mansion, complete with landscaped lakes, is the setting for this walk. The woodlands and lakes have become nature reserves, and parkland provides a pleasant site for the Yorkshire Sculpture Park.

3 Turn left and walk along the pavement to a road on your left which is signposted to the Litherop picnic site and High Hoyland. Go left along it to reach the picnic site on your left.

2 Continue through an iron gate along a woodland track to a crosstracks with a signpost. Turn left towards Bentley Grange. Reach the A636 and cross carefully to the pavement.

1 If you reach this walk by bus, start from the war memorial in West Bretton. This village is on the A637, 9 miles (14.5 km) east of Huddersfield, near junction 38 on the M1. Motorists should start at no. **4**.
Go up Park Lane to Bretton Hall and turn right just after its entrance, to follow a track into parkland. Emley Moor TV mast is on your left.

8 Motorists take the track on your left back to the car park. Otherwise go ahead for the bus stop.

7 Go ahead through a gate to pass playing-fields on your right. Ignore a signposted path to Clayton West on your left and keep straight ahead when a track forks right soon afterwards. Notice the totem pole and other exhibits in the Yorkshire Sculpture Park on your right. Follow the track to the entrance of Bretton Hall.

6 Cross the stile and turn left along part of the Cal-Der-Went Walk. When the track bends right, go straight ahead through a gate into the grounds of Bretton Hall. Bretton Lake Nature Reserve (no public access) is on both sides of your path. Go ahead across Cascade Bridge between the Upper Lake and the Lower Lake. Ignore a stile on your right and go ahead across another bridge, over the canalised River Dearne. Ignore a stile on the right.

5 Go ahead to cross a stile in the fence at the top of the field and continue across the next field. Aim just to the left of the trees ahead (crossing gallops) to a stile.

4 Leaving the Litherop picnic site (and car park for motorists) on your left, pass a farm and turn left along a signposted public footpath.

West Bretton

Park Lane

A637

River Dearne

Lower Lake

Upper Lake

Cal-Der-Went Walk

Ⓑ   Ⓐ

P

A Bretton Hall was built by Sir William Wentworth in 1720, and at present houses a College of Higher Education. Its grounds are now a country park, owned by the district council.

B The Yorkshire Sculpture Park.

The sculptors Henry Moore and Barbara Hepworth were both born locally and have works here. The Park opened in 1977.

HOLMFIRTH

3.5 miles (5.6 km) Moderate

0 _____ 1 mile

0 _____ 1 km

Characters and character abound in this delightful spot. Holmfirth is now famous as the location for the 'Last of the Summer Wine' television series. Before the First World War it had the potential to become Britain's film making centre. Instead, it concentrated on saucy picture postcards. Just over half a century earlier, when the Bilberry Reservoir burst its dam in 1852, the ensuing flood swept 81 people to their deaths in the town below.

4 *Go left along a track for about 0.75 mile (1.2 km) to Upperthong and turn right at a signpost along Lydgetts. Go ahead through a wooden stile and along the edge of a field to reach a walled track and turn right. Follow this track for about 0.75 mile (1.2 km) to reach a TV mast. Turn left downhill immediately after the mast to the main road (A6024). Cross over to the fire station and turn right. Pass The Postcard pub on the left, the Civic hall on the right, and go down the steps on your left opposite Hightown Lane. Turn right along Norridge Bottom and turn right to return to the start.*

3 *Turn right along the A635. Cross the road to the Postcard Museum. Go up the footpath from the car park on your left after the museum to walk through Victoria Park to Cooper Lane, on your right. Turn left uphill to the top of Cooper Lane. Go right along Holt Lane, uphill to a small T junction.*

1 *Start from the Tourist Information Centre at Holmfirth. This is by the traffic lights at the junction of the A635 and the A6024, 6 miles (9.7 km) south of Huddersfield. Car parks are signposted nearby, and bus stops are also within easy reach.*
Cross the A635 carefully to walk down Victoria Street. Divert left just before the bridge to see the mark on the wall of a butcher's shop recording the height of the Great Flood in 1852. Go on to see the Valley Theatre, one of the oldest cinemas in the country, before retracing your steps and going across the bridge to the church. Notice 'Sid's Cafe' of television fame nearby. Go past the church to the White Hart pub and notice the Amiens Column on the left, across the road. Turn left after it to pass the Post Office on your right. Take the path in the corner on your right and cross the foot-bridge to reach the A6024. Turn right along the main road, turn right again at The Postcard pub to go down Crown Lane to the market. Turn left along Market Street, then at the far end turn right into Bridge Lane. Cross the bridge and go up the steps on your left. Turn right down Station Road.

Upperthong

Holmfirth

2 *Veer left up Daisy Lane, and before reaching the church tower, fork left uphill, passing on your right the small square building known as T'owd Towzer, the old lock-up. Continue uphill, passing Church Terrace on the right and up Bunker Hill to reach Back Lane. Turn right, reach South Lane and turn sharply right downhill. Cross Dunford Road to Hinchcliffe's shop, and take the gap on the left past The Nook pub, cross over the stream to reach Hollowgate. Bear left along here, and at the far end cross the bridge to regain the main road (A635).*

A Look here for an intriguing legacy of the days of domestic textile production. 'Wuzzing holes' are shallow indentations, about as deep as a large finger. Rods used to be put in these holes so that baskets of wet wool could be 'wuzzed' or spun dried. Two such 'wuzzing holes' can be seen in a stone of the retaining wall on your right about 30 yards (27 m) up Bunkers Hill.

B The Postcard Museum offers free admission (Mon – Sat 10 – 5, Sun 1 – 5). Visit it to see the collection of saucy postcards made by the local firm of Bamforth's.

Walk 30

THE YORKSHIRE MINING MUSEUM

5.5 miles (8.9 km) Moderate

This walk will provide you with a welcome breath of fresh air either before or after a trip down a preserved coal-mine. The paths are good with part of the walk taking the waymarked route of the Kirklees Way. Fieldpaths, woodland paths and farm tracks are followed, and the views are extensive and interesting. Children under the age of five are not allowed down the coal-mine, and you are advised to wear old clothes.

4 *Turn right over a stile beside a gate and go ahead with a hedge on your right. Cross a stile into a wood. Keep near the wall on your right for 100 yards (90 m) then bear left. Cross a track to continue down a path to a stile in a wall. Go ahead to a signposted gate and turn left up a track. Reach a tennis court on your right.*

3 *Cross the foot-bridge and turn right to follow a fence on your right. Go ahead over a stile in the corner to follow a hedge on your right as it bears left. Cross a farm access track to continue beside a hedge on your right to another stile. Cross it to go left for a few paces.*

2 *Ignore the road up to the Reindeer Inn on your right. Go ahead 30 yards (27 m) and turn left through a gap in the wall. Take a path which bears left, then descends and bears right to a stile in the bottom right corner of this woodland. Cross the stile and turn left. Reach another stile and turn left over it.*

Overton

A642

Denby Wood

Woodlands Farm

Yorkshire Mining Museum (A) (P)

Grange Wood

A642

1 *The Yorkshire Mining Museum (parking) is on the A642 half way between Wakefield and Huddersfield with easy access from both the M1 and M62. Buses run to the nearby Reindeer Inn from Leeds, Huddersfield, Wakefield, Barnsley, Dewsbury and Overton. Go left along the A642 from the museum.*

New Hall Camp

5 *Turn left over a gate waymarked with a blue K, opposite the tennis court. Go ahead over another stile and downhill. Near the bottom, turn right over a stile in the wall and turn left to have the wall now on your left. Cross a foot-bridge and walk with a wood on your right. Cross a stile into the next field and go ahead to leave it by a turnstile in the corner.*

(B)

A637

Flockton

Mill Beck

Over

0   1 mile

0   1 km

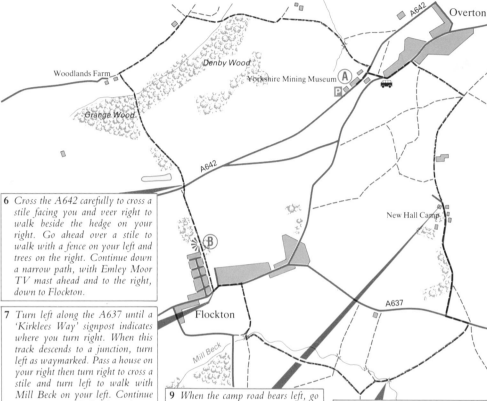

6 *Cross the A642 carefully to cross a stile facing you and veer right to walk beside the hedge on your right. Go ahead over a stile to walk with a fence on your left and trees on the right. Continue down a narrow path, with Emley Moor TV mast ahead and to the right, down to Flockton.*

7 *Turn left along the A637 until a 'Kirklees Way' signpost indicates where you turn right. When this track descends to a junction, turn left as waymarked. Pass a house on your right then turn right to cross a stile and turn left to walk with Mill Beck on your left. Continue over a waymarked stile and veer right to another stile. Go ahead to cross a third stile, then a concrete farm road and a fourth stile. Cross a fifth waymarked stile in the next hedge and walk with a hedge on your left until another stile appears in it. Turn left to walk down to Mill Beck and turn right downstream to a foot-bridge, which you turn left to cross.*

9 *When the camp road bears left, go straight ahead up a farm track. Continue past New Hall Farm and follow the track to a junction of five tracks. Take the second track on your left, going off at a right angle and soon passing a cricket ground on your right. Reach a road and cross it to turn left along the pavement. Fork right just before the Reindeer Inn to reach the Yorkshire Mining Museum.*

8 *Go uphill with a hedge on your left. When the hedge veers left, veer right towards a barn. Pass the barn on your right to join a track that leads to the A637. Cross this road carefully and turn left along the pavement, passing a water tower on your right. Turn right down a No Through Road and continue past New Hall Camp (Remand Centre).*

A The Yorkshire Mining Museum was opened in 1988 at the old Claphouse Colliery. Guided tours take you down 465 ft (142 m) every day of the year (except Christmas Day and New Year's Day) between 10 – 5. Allow plenty of time here.

B The TV mast you can see at Emley Moor is 1080 ft (329 m) high – the second tallest structure in England.

Walk 31
HURSTWOOD RESERVOIR
2 miles (3.2 km) Easy

0   1 mile

0   1 km

This is a short, easy stroll around Hurstwood Reservoir, one of the many reservoirs on the moors to the east of Burnley. It is screened from the village by conifer trees, which enhances the setting and prevents the erosion of soil on the steeper slopes. The walk is waymarked and has well maintained stiles and two foot-bridges along its route.

4 Go ahead over a stile when the wall on your left ends. Continue beside the fence on your right. Go ahead over the hummocky landscape above the head of the reservoir and look out for a foot-bridge in the bottom of the valley on your right.

5 Turn right to descend to the foot-bridge and use it to cross Hurstwood Brook.

6 Turn right along a track which takes you past the reservoir on your right.

3 Cross the stile ahead and bear left as directed by a waymark arrow. Keep the wall on your left as you bend right with the path.

2 Go ahead over the waymarked stile beside a gate. Go diagonally left towards the far corner of the field to a kissing gate. Continue with the wall on your left and trees behind a fence on your right.

7 Go ahead through the gate (or use the foot-bridge if locked) along the track through the conifer trees. Ignore a track to the dam on your right and another track on your left. Go straight ahead to return to the car park.

1 Start from the car park which is near the water treatment works at Hurstwood Reservoir. This is at the end of Hurstwood Lane about 1 mile (1.6 km) south of Worsthorne and 3 miles (4.8 km) east of Burnley. Worsthorne is the terminus of the nearest bus service (nos 3 and 4 from Burnley).
Walk back along Hurstwood Lane across the bridge to the telephone box. Turn right up the No Through Road.

A Hurstwood Reservoir dates back to 1925. It is located on Worsthorne Moor, which is one of the largest water catchment areas in the South Pennines. This and other reservoirs were constructed to provide the expanding town of Burnley with its water supply.

B This hummocky landscape is a result of earlier quarrying activity.

Walk 32
WORSTHORNE
3.5 miles (5.6 km) Moderate

The moors above Burnley provide interesting walks. Although they are mostly bare, it is possible to find pleasantly wooded cloughs. The trees would have covered a much larger area in prehistoric times, when the stone circle that can be seen near the end of this walk was constructed. Come on a fine day for the distant views, with Pendle Hill a landmark to the north.

3 Cross a stile and go straight ahead, following the well made path along the valley for 0.5 mile (0.8 km). Turn left when you are level with the base of the dam of Lee Green Reservoir, and climb the path keeping the hedge/fence to your left. Extwistle Hall is above you, to the left. Cross a stile in the corner of the field to emerge on the track. Turn right and continue to where it joins the lane.

4 Turn right just before the lane to take a track to Lee Green, where you turn left to reach the lane at Roggerham Gate Inn. Turn right down to where the lane bends sharply right.

5 Turn left through a gate and go ahead along a track. After about 300 yards (274 m) bear right up a wide, grassy path to cross a stile in the corner of two walls.

2 Turn right at a sharp left hand bend up the unmade Lennox Street and turn left at the end. Pass the recreation ground on your right. When you reach a track junction, turn right and follow this track to Wood Hey Farm. Passing to the front of the farm, go slightly left and cross over a stile. Go ahead about 100 yards (91 m) to a waymark post and turn right to a wooded clough (valley). Cross the stream by stepping stones.

1 Start from the village green at Worsthorne. This is the terminus of the nos 3 and 4 bus services from Burnley. Worsthorne is about 3 miles (4.8 km) east of Burnley. Cars can be parked near the green. Leave the village green by Brownside Road.

7 Turn right down this track which takes you straight back to Worsthorne. Pass the church on your left before reaching the village green.

6 Head for the top left hand corner of the next field, walking roughly parallel to a line of pylons on the left. Continue beside a wall on your left to reach a track junction.

Map labels: Extwistle Hall · Lee Green · Swinden Bridge · Swinden Reservoirs · (A) · (D) · Lee Green Reservoir · Swinden Water · Ring Stones · (B) · (C) · Slipper Hill · Worsthorne · Church · P

A Extwistle Hall was built in the late 16th century. Its interior was badly damaged by a gunpowder explosion in 1717.

B Just before the end of the first field, notice a rough area on the other side of the wire fence. This was a prehistoric enclosure.

C Half way down, the second field, notice an old steam roller and some old farm machinery on your right. On the other side of this can be found an ancient stone circle, comprised of five stones. They are very low but can be easily distinguished.

D The remains of an early textile mill.

53

Walk 33

PENDLE HERITAGE CENTRE

5 miles (8 km) Easy

Pendle Country, in Lancashire, has a special charm of its own. A visit to the Pendle Heritage Centre is essential to fully enjoy this. The Centre is in a 17th-century farmhouse that was the home of the ancestors of the athlete Roger Bannister in more recent times. You won't need to be that athletic to complete this walk, however, as it is fairly level. Rivers followed to roads, which in t lead to a canal.

A The rocky bed of Pendle Water was a 'stannery' that supplied road stone centuries ago.

B 'Th'Owd Brig' was built in 1583. When packhorses used it, it didn't have a parapet, in order that wide loads could be carried over. In the 1770s, John Wesley, the founder of Methodism, preached from here.

C The Pendle Way is a 45 mile (72 km) circular walk from the Pendle Heritage Centre via Barnoldswick and Wycoller. It returns to the Centre over Pendle Hill. Its distinctive witch waymark is a reminder of the Pendle Witches in the 17th century. This route was opened in 1987.

D Blacko Tower has the look of Glastonbury Tor about it. It was erected in 1890 by an eccentric local grocer and landowner, Joseph Stanfield, who was disappointed when he found that it didn't give him a view of the Ribble Valley.

E Just before the second bridge over the canal, notice the former Wanless Wharf. This jetty was used to unload cotton, coal and other goods for Colne. The navvies who dug the canal were catered for by a pub, The Grinning Rat, opened in the farmhouse opposite.

F This is the Leeds and Liverpool Canal. At 127 miles (204 km), it is the longest in the country. It took 46 years to build, from 1770 to 1816. When it was completed, it ensured the growth of the cotton industry which revolutionised the towns and villages of East Lancashire.

G The canal section between Barrowford and Barnoldswick was opened in 1796 and remains the highest point in the system, at 487 feet (148 m). The seven Barrowford Locks enabled barges to descend the 69 feet (21 m) towards Nelson. The reservoir helps to replace the 60,000 gallons (272,760 litres) used by each lock operation.

H The Pendle Heritage Centre is open from Easter to the last Sunday in Nov, on Tues, Wed, Thurs, Sat, Sun and Bank Holiday Mon from 2 – 4.30. The 17th-century farmhouse contains displays about the Pendle area and its witches. Outside is an ancient cruck barn and a walled garden with old-fashioned flowers and vegetables. An 18th-century ba houses a heritage shop and room (admission charge).

Pendle had long been known its witches. The famous Pend witch trials took place in 1612. T local farmers knew to give a tri to the wandering old women w called on them as beggars. If th weren't careful, some bad lu might befall them. The authorit were keen to root out all witche and none was keener than Rog Newell, the local magistra Inexplicable incidents, such as t bewitching of a cow which Jo Nutter had asked Moth Demdike, a feared witch, to cu told against them. Old Demdi admitted to being an agent of t devil and told of causing a murd by sticking pins in a clay effig Roger Newell acquired t evidence he wanted to hear a rounded up more witches. As result, 10 witches from the Pend area were executed in 1612 (nine Lancaster and one at York). A outbreak of witchcraft in 16 almost led to 17 more local peop being executed, but they we reprieved. The clerk to the judg of Lancaster Assizes, Thom Potts, left his own record of t trial of these witches, which was inspire later romantic novelists.

Ov

0   1 mile
0   1 km

4 Go ahead over two stiles, keeping the river on your left, to reach a lane. Ignore the bridge on your left and turn right up the lane to reach a crossroads. Go ahead towards Nelson along the pavement beside the A682. Pass through Blacko, with the tower on the hill on your left. Leave the A682 to fork left down Beverley Road and continue along this to the Cross Gaits Inn.

3 Reach Watermeetings, the confluence of Blacko Water and Pendle Water. Turn right over the bridge here and turn left immediately. Veer right to cross another foot-bridge on your left. Veer right from this to a stile. There is a fine view of Blacko Tower on top of the hill to your right. Go straight ahead to a stile and walk with a wall on your right to a farm. Take the waymarked path to a road and turn right down it. Just after the road crosses a bridge, turn left to follow the river on your left.

5 Go ahead across Barnoldswick Road at the road junction and take the signposted public footpath facing you. Walk with a hedge on your right and go over stiles and past three fields on your left. Continue over a stile to a fenced path ahead and follow this across a foot-bridge over a stream coming from your right. Go ahead along a shady path to emerge before a bridge over a canal. Go ahead across this bridge and turn left to the canal. Turn left again immediately to follow the towpath under the bridge with the canal on your right.

Blacko

Ⓓ

Beverley

Black o Water

A682

Pendle Water

Higherford

Leeds & Liverpool Canal

Ⓔ

Ⓕ

2 Turn left across the bridge and turn right immediately to go up the lane past an old bridge on your right. Go ahead at the end of the lane along the Pendle Way (waymarked with a witch on a broomstick) with the river on your right.

Ⓒ

Ⓑ

Ⓖ

6 Follow the canal towpath under another bridge. Continue to pass the Barrowford Locks on your right and Barrowford Reservoir on your left. Ignore the foot-bridges across the ends of each lock, but go under a new road bridge and turn right over an old road bridge after the fifth lock. Another road bridge, carrying the M65, is now on your left. Go up the track between the M65 on your left and the B6247 on your right to reach a stile beside a gate on your right. This is waymarked with the Pendle Way's witch on a broomstick.

1 Start from the Pendle Heritage Centre at Barrowford. This is on the B6247 near its junction with the A682 about 1 mile (1.6 km) north of junction 13 on the M65. There is a car park across the road from the Centre. If you come by bus, take nos 9 or 10 to Barrowford Park from Burnley (via Nelson). Start by crossing the stile beside the gate at the back of the car park to walk with the river (Pendle Water) on your left.

Barrowford Reservoir

Ⓐ

Ⓟ

A682

Ⓗ

B6247

M65

Barrowford

7 Cross the stile and turn left along the pavement of the Colne Road (the B6247) back to the Pendle Heritage Centre (on your left – the car park is on your right).

HOLLINGWORTH LAKE

5 miles (8 km) Easy

| 0 | | | | 1 mile |
| 0 | | 1 km | | |

This is an easy walk, where Victorian ladies used to stroll wearing their most elegant clothes. It can be shortened by starting from the Visitor Centre car park. There's plenty to see, with coots, moorhens, snipe, mallard and great crested grebe usually on the water. The country park is one of the most popular in England and its Visitor Centre houses a fine exhibition.

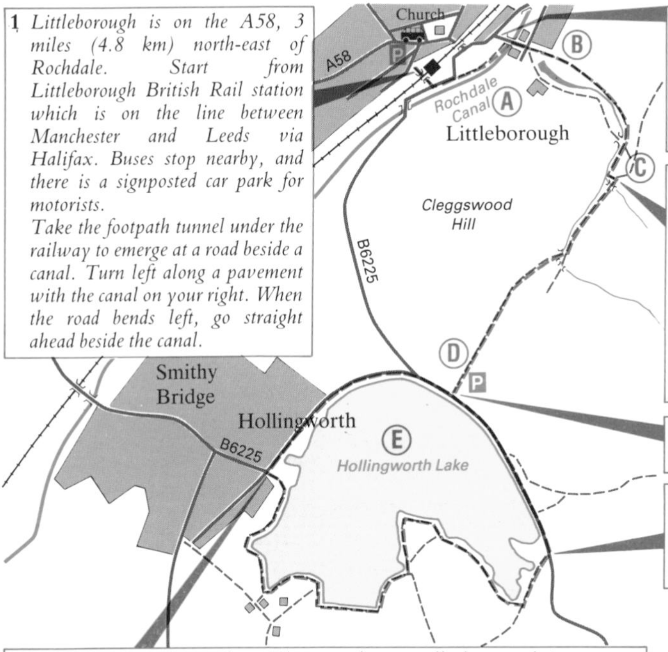

1 *Littleborough is on the A58, 3 miles (4.8 km) north-east of Rochdale. Start from Littleborough British Rail station which is on the line between Manchester and Leeds via Halifax. Buses stop nearby, and there is a signposted car park for motorists.*
Take the footpath tunnel under the railway to emerge at a road beside a canal. Turn left along a pavement with the canal on your right. When the road bends left, go straight ahead beside the canal.

2 *Turn right at the first bridge you reach (by a lock). Cross it and go ahead up a path to a road. Cross this road to take the lane facing you, passing Courtaulds on your right.*

3 *When you reach a signpost, turn right over a foot-bridge across a stream. Follow the signposted path to Hollingworth Lake, walking with the stream on your right to a foot-bridge on your right. Cross this to continue past a picnic site on your left and go ahead to the Visitor Centre. Continue to the lake.*

4 *Turn left to walk with the lake on your right.*

5 *Turn right along the signposted path into Hollingworth Lake Country Park. Continue with the lake on your right.*

6 *You return to the road at The Beach Tavern and go right with the lake on your right. When you have walked around it, retrace your steps past the Visitor Centre to Littleborough.*

Map labels: Church, A58, P, Littleborough, Rochdale Canal (A), (B), (C), Cleggswood Hill, B6225, Smithy Bridge, Hollingworth, B6225, Hollingworth Lake (E), (D), P

A The Rochdale Canal linked the Calder and Hebble Navigation at Sowerby Bridge with the Bridgewater Canal in Manchester. It was the first and most successful of the three trans-Pennine canals. First proposed in 1766, work didn't start on it until 1794 and the section from Sowerby Bridge to Rochdale was opened in 1798, followed by the extension into Manchester in 1804. Its 33 miles (53.1 km) needed 92 locks and its construction was a remarkable piece of engineering. Sadly, it closed to traffic above Manchester in 1952, but it is now being restored.

B Ealees was an old community with its own mill when the canal was being surveyed in the 1780s.

C Coal used to be dug out of the hillside here.

D The Visitor Centre.

E A huge amount of water was needed for the Rochdale Canal, and Hollingworth Lake became the largest reservoir to supply it in 1798. It covers 118 acres (47.8 hectares) and is now popular for sailing.

BLACKSTONE EDGE

4.5 miles (7.2 km) Strenuous

Dramatic views from the summit of Blackstone Edge make this an excellent walk. Take care to keep to the described route, which is easy to follow.

5 *Walk along the broad, grassy track. It descends gradually and bears left before curving right. Pass a flooded quarry on your left and bear left to reach the A58 at another bus stop (for nos 564, 567 and 568). Cross the road carefully and pass Bar House on your left as you go down Blackstone Edge Old Road and back to the start.*

4 *Cross the bridge and turn right to walk with the water channel on your right. Follow the waymarked Pennine Way when it forks left just before a gate ahead. Descend to the A58, cross it carefully and go right towards The White House. Turn sharply left to take the signposted bridleway just before you reach The White House.*

Blackstone Edge Moor

Roman Road

Lydgate

Robin Hood's Bed

472m

Blackstone Edge

1 *Start from the bus stop at Lydgate, 1 mile (1.6 km) east of Littleborough (British Rail station). The road is crossed by electricity pylons at this point and there is space for car parking. The buses serving this stop are the no. 564 between Halifax and Littleborough and the no. 568 between Halifax and Rochdale. Take the track beside the houses on your right, forking right off the road. Continue with a wall on your right.*

2 *Pass a lay-by beside the A58 on your left. Continue walking uphill with a wall on your right, ignoring a track to Blackstone Edge Farm on your right. You soon step onto the famous 'Roman' road. Follow this uphill to the distinctive, waymarked, Aiggin Stone on your left.*

3 Take great care to remember your route now as you will be retracing your steps. *Turn right along the Pennine Way, crossing peat to reach the rocks of Blackstone Edge. An Ordnance Survey column is erected on a huge boulder. About 30 yards (27 m) further on is the rock known as Robin Hood's Bed. Retrace your steps from here to the Aiggin Stone. Turn left down the 'Roman' road to a foot-bridge over a reservoir feeder channel.*

A This paved road is thought by many to be Roman. It could have formed part of the route between Mancunium (Manchester) and Olicana (Ilkley). If it is Roman, then this stretch is remarkably well preserved.

B The Aiggin Stone is a guide stone marking the summit of the old road.

C There is a fine view from the 1548 ft (472 m) summit of Blackstone Edge. Robin Hood came from these parts and was outlawed to Sherwood Forest.

DIGGLE

4 miles (6.4 km) Easy

0   1 mile

0   1 km

Industrial archaeology, in the midst of pleasant scenery, is the focus of attention on this walk. A towpath leads you to the mouth of Standedge Tunnel, the highest and longest canal tunnel in the British Isles. Its construction was an epic engineering achievement. Opened in 1811, the tunnel was closed in 1944. There is hope of it reopening in the future.

5 Retrace your steps to the canal and walk back on the other bank, with the canal on your left. When you reach an old lock before J. Barrett's, turn left across the canal to return to the towpath of your outward route. Retrace your steps to Saddleworth Museum.

4 Go ahead up a lane and turn right to stand on a bridge over the railway. Notice the tunnel entrances on your left. From left to right these are the 1894 railway tunnel (still in use), the 1811 canal tunnel, the 1849 railway tunnel and the 1871 railway tunnel.

2 Cross the bridge on your right and continue along the towpath with the canal on your left.

3 Follow the canal towpath under Saddleworth Viaduct. Keep to the right of the canal until you reach the A670. Cross this road carefully and take the public footpath signposted to Diggle. This soon reverts to being the towpath of the canal, which is on your left again. Keep the canal on your left until the water ends at Diggle.

1 Start from Saddleworth Museum. This is in Uppermill, on the A670, 5 miles (8 km) east of Oldham. There is a car park at the museum (and other car parks nearby). Bus no. 365 runs to here from Oldham, Manchester and Huddersfield. The nearest railway station is at Greenfield, on the line between Manchester and Huddersfield. The towpath of the Huddersfield Narrow Canal links this station with the museum, adding 1 mile (1.6 km) in each direction.

Go ahead from the museum entrance to pass the gardens, turn right to a signpost and follow the towpath of the canal, which is now on your right, in the direction of Diggle.

A Visit Saddleworth Museum before going on the walk. It provides a valuable introduction to this area, and to the canal in particular. Among its exhibits are tenterposts, used to stretch cloth while drying.

B Saddleworth Viaduct was erected in the late 1840s.

C Diggle lies at the southern end of the Standedge canal and rail tunnels. The canal tunnel is 5698 yards (5210 m) long and boats had to be 'legged' through, the boatmen lying on the boat and walking it along the walls.

Walk 37
WHITWORTH
4.5 miles (7.2 km) Easy

0   1 mile

0   1 km

The waymarked Rossendale Way forms the bulk of this route, so the path is well defined. The walk is fairly flat, with only gradual climbs along old tracks. The line of the dismantled railway provides an easy route out of Whitworth and its viaduct gives a spectacular crossing of the nature reserve at Healey Dell Gorge.

1 *Start from the Dog & Partridge Inn at the junction of Market Street and Church Street in Whitworth. This is on the A671, 3 miles (4.8 km) north of Rochdale, from where there are* buses (nos. 464, 466 and 467). *Two car parks are signposted nearby. Cross the road to the telephone box and go ahead up Hall Street.*

2 *Turn left along Wallbank Drive. As you pass a small lake on your left turn right up a footpath to join a bridleway. Turn left and follow this around the back of the Wallbank Estate. This bears left, passes a mill and joins a dismantled railway. Turn right here and follow the path.*

3 *Continue past the site of Broadley Station, where the old platform is on your right. Ignore the former station approach lane which branches off up a ramp to the left. Go ahead under a bridge and over a viaduct which provides a magnificent view over a wooded valley. At the end of the viaduct, turn left down steps, then turn right up a road.*

4 *Reach the A671 at Healey and cross it carefully to go ahead up Ending Rake, the lane opposite. Go through an arch and continue with a wall on your right.*

5 *Go ahead along the lane past cottages on your left. When the concrete road turns right, go ahead along a waymarked path with a wall on your right.*

6 *Bear left along the waymarked path. Keep left at a fork. Leave the Rossendale Way at the next crosstracks, where you turn left along a lane back to Whitworth. Pass the church and The Red Lion on your right. Go along Taylor Street to reach Church Street and the start of the walk.*

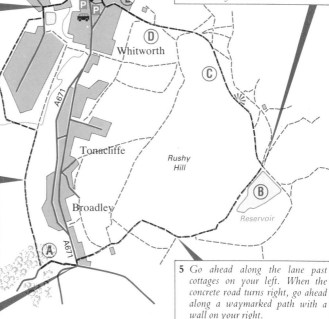

A This magnificent viaduct was built in 1866 to carry the Lancashire and Yorkshire Railway from Rochdale to Whitworth. The line was closed in 1967, but the viaduct still gives fine views over the wooded Healey Dell Gorge.

B Hamer Pasture Reservoir was built in 1846 to supply Rochdale with water. Unfortunately, it leaked and is now disused.

C Lord Byron used to admire the view from this track with his lover, Mary Ann Chaworth.

D Lobden Golf Course is on the site of the ancient Whitworth Rushbearing festivities.

E Whitworth used to be famous for its doctors. Their patients came great distances and found lodgings in the village.

59

Walk 38
BACUP
2.5 miles (4 km) Easy

Bacup town centre is a Lancashire cotton town. In its Anglia. Coal was also mined here Conservation Area of special heyday workers flocked to Bacup's and this walk passes old mines. architectural and historical interest. mills from as far away as East Visitors may recognise it as It is recognised as being the best 'Hartley' of the 'Juliet Bravo' remaining example of a small television series.

4 *Turn left along the track known as Old Meadows Lane, with a wall on your right. Continue under the arch of an old bridge which carried a farm road in the early 19th century. Pass a farmhouse on your left and go ahead to a second farmhouse, 'Brow Top'.*

5 *Turn right at 'Brow Top' to walk uphill with a wall on your left. Go ahead across the corner at the top of the field and cross a stile in the wall ahead.*

6 *Go straight ahead and veer right, through a gap in the wall ahead, to cross into the next field. Maintain this direction, aiming for the top of the second field on your right. Cross a step stile in the wall and go ahead with a wall on your right. Veer left to a stile beside a gate which gives access to a lane, Todmorden Old Road.*

3 *Go ahead to the first turn on the right (Blackthorn Lane) and go right along it. Just before the cricket ground, turn left up Cowtoot Lane. Pass a school on your right and go ahead up a track to a junction.*

7 *Turn right down Todmorden Old Road. Emerge at Greensnook Lane, where you turn left towards the church. Bear right down to the A681 (Todmorden Road) and turn right along its pavement back to Yorkshire Street and the Natural History Museum. Look out for the stocks outside the Health Centre on your left.*

2 *Follow the pavement of Burnley Road until you reach Cooper Street on your right. Turn right here and notice where the River Irwell starts its culverted journey under Bacup on your left.*

1 *Start from the Natural History Museum in Yorkshire Street, Bacup. This is on the A681 near its junction with the A671, between Rochdale and Burnley. There are several car parks signposted, and buses stop nearby,* *including the R33 from Todmorden, (where there is a railway station). Walk to the right to reach the roundabout in the centre of Bacup and bear right up Burnley Road.*

A Bacup's Natural History Museum is only open on Thursday evenings (7.30 – 10). Admission is free and there are many interesting exhibits.

B The cricket groud dates back to 1860 and reflects the Saturday afternoon holiday gained by the 1847 Ten Hour Day Act.

C Old Meadows Colliery was the last National Coal Board pit in Rossendale until it closed in 1969.

D This was the main road to Yorkshire until the 19th century.

E Opencast coal mining was carried out here in 1956 and 1957.

F Christ Church was built in 1854.

G These stocks were used from 1749 to 1850. Also outside this Health Centre is a Crushing Circle (once used to crush rock), rescued from a local quarry.

H Devotees of the BBC television series 'Juliet Bravo' will want to see Bacup's police station, which featured in the programmes.

Walk 39

TODMORDEN

2.5 miles (4 km) Easy

Todmorden was the home of 'Honest John' Fielden. Elected MP for Oldham in 1832, he obtained the Ten Hour Day Act in 1847, arguing that a shorter working day would lead to greater efficiency, as well as fewer accidents. This walk passes places associated with him.

6 Turn right over the stile and descend with a fence on your right to a small gate. Turn right to walk with a wall on your right. Ignore a stile in it, but cross a stile ahead. Descend with a fence on your right to a lane. Go ahead down a path to a church.

7 Continue to the A646 and turn right along its pavement. Go under the railway viaduct and turn right, back to the start.

1 Start at the Tourist Information Centre, Todmorden. This is near the railway station (on the line from Leeds to Manchester via Halifax), the bus station and car parks. The A646 joins the A6033 here.
Go right, passing the Town Hall on your left. Go ahead along the Rochdale Road, crossing the canal.

2 Look out for a Calderdale Way waymark on your right and turn right up a rough track named Dobroyd Road. Cross a bridge over the canal and continue, with great care, across the railway crossing.

3 Bear left following the lane. Go straight ahead across the road leading into the grounds of Dobroyd Castle (now a school). Reach a hairpin bend and go ahead through a gap in the wall on your left to follow a footpath uphill.

4 Turn right along a walled track. Pass a TV mast on your right. Ignore the first turning on your right, but turn right along the second, which is a grassy track with a wall on both sides. Notice an ancient standing stone in the field on your left.

5 Go round the corner on your right and turn left along the waymarked Calderdale Way, crossing a stile beside a gate. Dobroyd Castle can soon be seen below you on the right. Following Pinghold, leave the Calderdale Way by crossing a stile beside a gate. Go ahead beside a wall on your right for 70 yards (64 m) to a stile.

A Todmorden Town Hall was funded by Samuel, John and Joshua Fielden, the sons of 'Honest John' Fielden. It was designed by John Gibson and opened in 1875.

B This ancient standing stone must have given its name to Stones, the house close by, where Jenny Greenwood, the mother of 'Honest John' Fielden, used to live before marrying her neighbour and fellow Quaker, Joshua Fielden.

C Dobroyd Castle was built in 1869 by Honest John. Fielden's son John, who became a member of the landed gentry. It is now a school.

D Joshua Fielden sold Edge End in 1782 to start his cotton business, two years before 'Honest John' was born.

E Todmorden is in Yorkshire, but part of it was in Lancashire until 1888 and Lancashire League cricket is still played here.

WALSDEN

3 miles (4.8 km) Moderate

The Industrial Revolution turned this remote valley into a corridor for canal, railway and road. All three means of transport can be seen from this walk, but it is the rugged beauty that still prevails. The Celts must have found shelter here when the English conquered this land, since Walsden is derived from Walsh or Welsh, meaning 'foreigner' in Old English.

1 *Start from the Waggon & Horses Inn on the A6033 at the southern end of Walsden and 2 miles (3.2 km) south of Todmorden's railway* station. *Cars can be parked near the pub, and buses from Todmorden stop here. With your back to the Waggon &* Horses Inn, *turn right towards a bus shelter. Veer right up a walled path just before the shelter. Reach a farm road and bear right along it.*

2 *Follow the farm road around a hairpin bend. Pass Lower Allescholes Farm on your left, then Higher Allescholes on your right.*

3 *Follow the lane as it bends left. Pass the turning to Moor Hey Farm on your right and go ahead along a rough track to a gate. Keep to this rough track until it approaches electricity pylons.*

4 *Just before you reach the pylons, turn left to descend to a lower path. Turn left along this path and soon pass an air shaft of the railway tunnel.*

5 *Gradually descend with a fine view across the canal on your right. Pass a second air shaft.*

9 *Turn sharply left along a path to the railway. Cross this carefully, then cross a foot-bridge and bear left to the A6033. Turn right to return to the start of the walk.*

8 *Turn left to walk with the canal on your right. Reach Lightbank Lock and go ahead 50 yards (46 m).*

7 *Reach the A6033 and cross this road carefully. Turn left along its pavement and ignore the first path on your right, which takes a bridge over the canal. Turn right by the seat down steps to join the towpath near Bottomley Lock.*

6 *Continue through a gate to pass a third air shaft. Go through another gate and turn right.*

A These are the air shafts of the railway tunnel. George Stephenson built the railway through this Summit Tunnel, which was opened on 11th December, 1840. This line connects Manchester and Leeds via Todmorden, and was planned as early as 1825, although building didn't start until 1837. Work started on the tunnel in 1838, and was an immense task, requiring 1000 men, 100 horses and 13 stationary steam engines. It is lined with 23 million bricks and 8000 tons of cement. The tunnel's length of 1.75 miles (2.8km) made it, for a while, the longest railway tunnel in the world. When it was almost finished, there was a rumour that it had collapsed. George Stephenson took the owners to see that an earth movement had caused very little damage. He wagered his reputation that nothing could destroy the strong linings. He was proved right when a petrol-tanker train caught fire in the tunnel in December 1984, sending burning gas shooting from the ventilator shafts like volcanoes.

B The Rochdale Canal was the first of the three trans-Pennine canals, being completed in 1802. Its 33 miles (53 km) required 92 locks. This canal linked the Calder and Hebble Navigation at Sowerby Bridge with the Bridgewater Canal at Manchester. It was abandoned in 1952 but many miles have now been restored.